CROSS STITCH

TIMELESS Treasures™

Publisher: Donna Robertson
Design Director: Fran Rohus
Production Director: Ange Workman

EDITORIAL
Senior Editor: Janet Tipton
Associate Editors: Kim Pierce, Marianne Telesca
Text & Graphics Composing Editors: Nancy Harris,
Pauline Rosenberger

PRODUCTION
Production Manager: Jean Schrecengost
Book Design: Betty Gibbs Radla
Cover Design: Glenda Chamberlain

PRODUCT DESIGN
Design Coordinator: Brenda Wendling

PHOTOGRAPHY
Cover Photo: Rusty Lingle
Stylist & Coordinator: Ruth Whitaker
Photographers: Mary Craft, Tammy Cromer-Campbell

BUSINESS
C.E.O.: John Robinson
Vice President Customer Service: Karen Pierce
Vice President Marketing: Greg Deily
Vice President M.I.S.: John Trotter

ACKNOWLEDGMENTS
Sincerest thanks to all the designers, stitchers and
professionals whose dedication has made this book possible.
Grateful acknowledgment to all of those who allowed
location shots on their properties. Thanks, also, to
David Norris and Kaye Stafford of Quebecor
Printing Book Group, Kingsport, TN.
Special thanks to the following manufacturers for supplying
materials for the projects featured in this book:
DMC • Zweigart® • Charles Craft, Inc. • Kreinik
Rhode Island Textiles • Anchor/J. & P. Coats
Wichelt Imports, Inc. • Taylor's Workshop
Anne Brinkley Designs • Daniel Enterprises • Janlynn®
Yarn Tree Designs • The New Berlin Co.
Ad Tech™ • V.I.P. Fabrics

Library of Congress Cataloging-in-Publication Data
ISBN: 1-57367-053-7
First Printing: 1996
Library of Contress Catalogue Number: 95-72039
Published and Distributed by
The Needlecraft Shop, LLC., Big Sandy, TX 75755
Printed in the United States of America

Introduction

Long ago needlework came into being as a way of binding skins and fabrics together for clothing and other protective gear. Artisans appeared among the most highly skilled stitchers, and needlework became more than a survival related craft. The archives of more than one ancient civilization have been recorded in stitches. Ancient Peruvian historians recorded the daily activities of temple life, weaving and embroidering pictographs onto elaborate textiles.

Stitchery skills – including the benefits of eye-to-hand coordination that needlework provides – continue to be passed from mother to daughter as they have been for thousands of years. But the reasons for sitting by the fire with hoop and needle have changed. Most of us purchase ready-made clothing and housing, and we have computers and statisticians for record keeping.

But needlework will not fade from popularity, because we need so much more than to just survive. The primal need we all possess for artistic expression is fully satisfied in cross stitch – fabric and thread, needle and light become the canvas, paint, brush and vision experienced in the painter's palette.

Time – the cherished moments of our lives – is the most precious gift we have to share with those we love. Feel the tug of the ancient weaver's thread. Leaf through the pages of Timeless Treasures, and stitch a page of history all your own.

Bequeath a generous endowment of love to generations to come.

Contents

Granny's Kitchen

Precious Years

Tiny Touches

Words of Wisdom

Family Ties

Strengthen the bonds of love
for your family when you
stitch commemorative
samplers and other
precious gifts.
Like a page from an old
family Bible, your
needlework will establish
your personal heritage to
live on from generation
to generation …
each stitch, a precious
memory in the heart of
someone you love.

Children Learn

A Child Learns What
He Lives

If a child lives with encouragement,
he learns confidence.
If a child lives with praise,
he learns to appreciate.
If a child lives with fairness,
he learns justice.
If a child lives with security,
he learns to have faith.
If a child lives with approval,
he learns to like himself.
If a child lives with acceptance,
and friendship,
he learns to find love in the
world.

Instructions on next page

Children Learn

DESIGNED BY EVE ANDRADE

MATERIALS:

18" x 21" piece of white 14-count Aida

INSTRUCTIONS:

1: Center and stitch design, using two strands floss for Cross Stitch. Use two strands floss for Backstitch of lettering and one strand floss for remaining Backstitch.❖

Stitch Count:
146 wide x 178 high

Approximate Design Size:
11-count 13⅜" x 16¼"
14-count 10½" x 12¾"
16-count 9⅛" x 11⅛"
18-count 8⅛" x 9⅞"
22-count 6⅝" x 8⅛"

X	B'st	¼x	DMC	ANCHOR	J.&P. COATS	COLORS
			#445	#288	#2288	Lemon Lt.
			#519	#168	#7168	Wedgewood Lt.
			#747	#928	#7167	Sky Blue
			#776	#24	#3281	Pink Med. Lt.
			#799	#136	#7030	Blue
			#816	#20	#3410	Christmas Red Red Very Dk.
			#828	#158	#7053	Larkspur Lt.
			#899	#55	#3282	Rose Med.
			#938	#381	#5477	Coffee Brown Ultra Dk.
			#950	#376	#2336	Terra Cotta Very Lt.
			#3350	#59	#3004	Dusty Rose Very Dk.
			#3750	#164	#7981	Navy Blue

X	B'st	¼x	¾x	DMC	ANCHOR	J.&P. COATS	COLORS
				#312	#979	#7979	Navy Blue Lt.
				#321	#47	#3500	Christmas Red
				#322	#978	#7978	Navy Blue Very Lt.
				#335	#38	#3238	Rose
				#367	#217	#6018	Pistachio Green Dk.
				#368	#214	#6016	Pistachio Green Lt.
				#407	#914	#5345	Spice Med.
				#414	#235	#8513	Steel Grey Med.
				#415	#398	#8510	Pearl Grey Very Lt.
				#433	#310	#5471	Coffee Brown
				#435	#901	#5371	Topaz Very Ultra Dk.
				#436	#890	#5943	Tan Brown
				#437	#362	#5942	Tan Brown Lt.

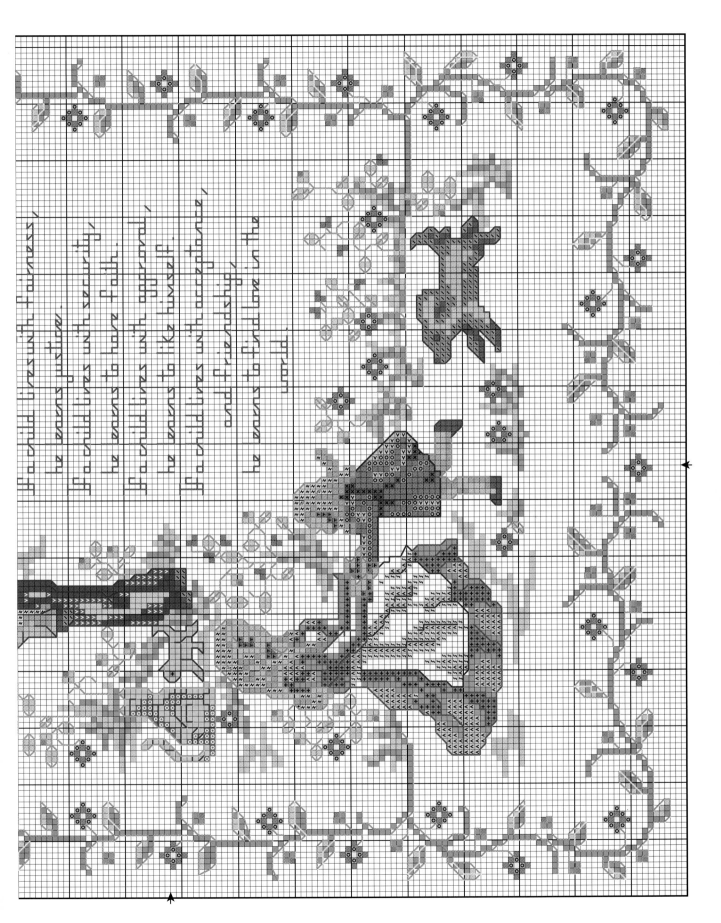

Wedding Roses

DESIGNED BY KATHLEEN HURLEY

MATERIALS:

16" x 16" piece of carnation pink 28-count Jubilee

INSTRUCTIONS:

1: Choosing letters and numbers of choice from Alphabet & Numbers graph, center and stitch design, stitching over two threads and using two strands floss for Cross Stitch and Backstitch of letters. Use one strand floss for remaining Backstitch.❖

595

Alphabet & Numbers

Stitch Count:
132 wide x 142 high

Approximate Design Size:
11-count 12" x 13"
14-count 9½" x 10¼"
16-count 8¼" x 8⅞"
18-count 7⅜" x 8"
22-count 6" x 6½"
28-count over two
  threads 9½" x 10¼"

X	B'st	DMC	ANCHOR	JPC	COLORS
◼	╱	#326	#39	#3401	Rose Ultra Deep
◪	╱	#367	#217	#6018	Pistachio Green Dk.
▦		#368	#214	#6016	Pistachio Green Lt.
⊞		#369	#259	#6015	Pistachio Green Very Lt.
☐		#726	#295	#2294	Topaz Lt.
◉		#776	#24	#3281	Pink Med.
		#818	#271	#3280	Baby Pink Lt.
		#890	#246	#6021	Pistachio Green Ultra Dk.
		#899	#55	#3282	Rose Med.

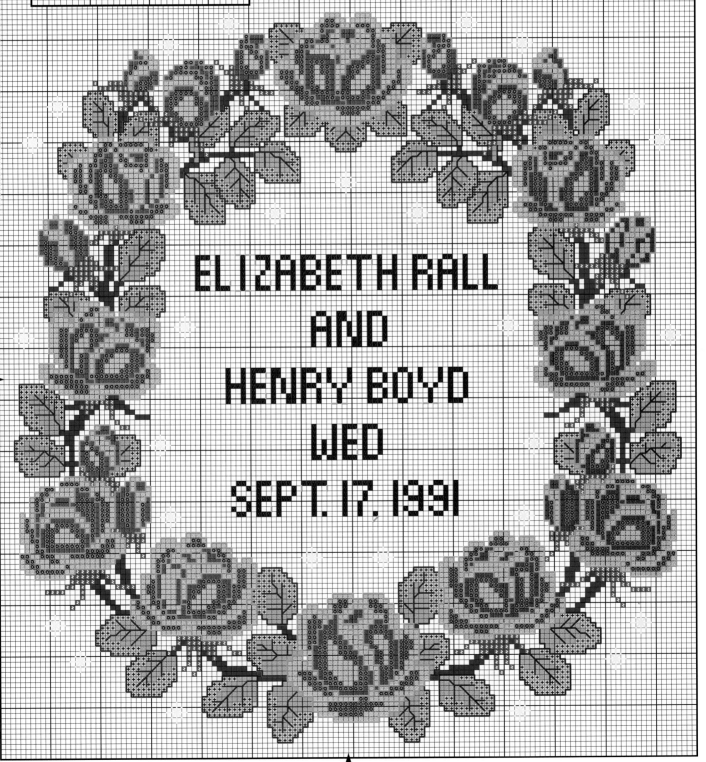

ELIZABETH RALL AND HENRY BOYD WED SEPT. 17, 1991

FAMILY TIES

11

Happy Home

Instructions on next page

Happy Home

Designed by Judy Chrispens

MATERIALS:

14" x 24" piece of blush 14-count Aida

INSTRUCTIONS:

1: Center and stitch design, using two strands floss for Cross Stitch and one strand floss for Backstitch. ❖

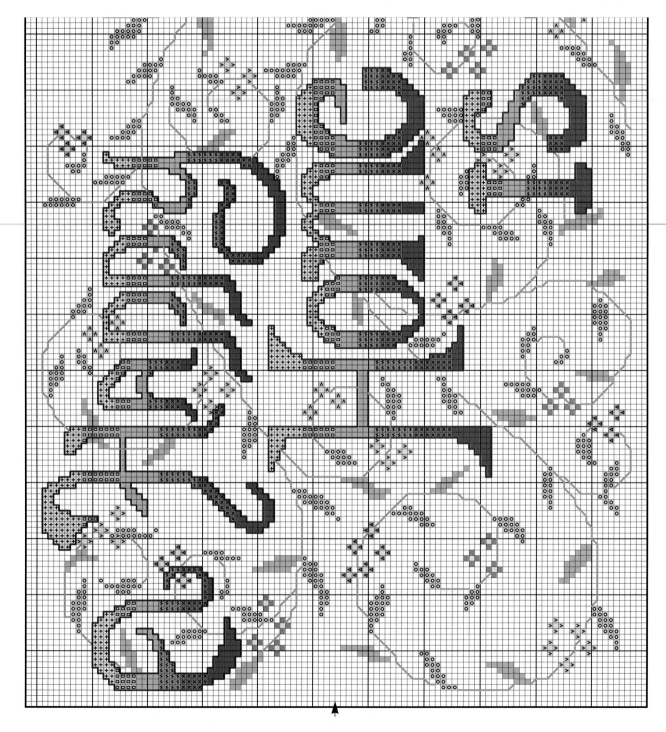

Stitch Count:
245 wide x 106 high

**Approximate
Design Size:**
11-count 22⅜" x 9⅝"
14-count 17½" x 7⅝"
16-count 15⅜" x 6⅝"
18-count 13⅝" x 6"
22-count 11⅛" x 4⅞"

X	B'st	DMC	ANCHOR	J.&P. COATS	COLORS
∨		#211	#342	#4303	Lavender Lt.
☐		#745	#300	#2296	Yellow Pale
☒		#796	#133	#7100	Royal Blue Dk.
⋈		#797	#132	#7023	Blue Med.
▦		#798	#131	#7022	Cornflower Blue Dk.
▣		#799	#136	#7030	Blue
⊞		#800	#129	#7020	Delft Pale
◼	╱	#820	#134	#7024	Royal Blue Very Dk.
	╱	#986	#246	#6021	Pistachio Green Ultra Dk.
▨		#987	#244	#6258	Willow Green
○		#989	#242	#6266	Apple Green
▲		#3341	#328	#3008	Peach Flesh
▷		#3689	#49	#3086	Mauve Lt.
◼		#3731	#77	#3283	Rose

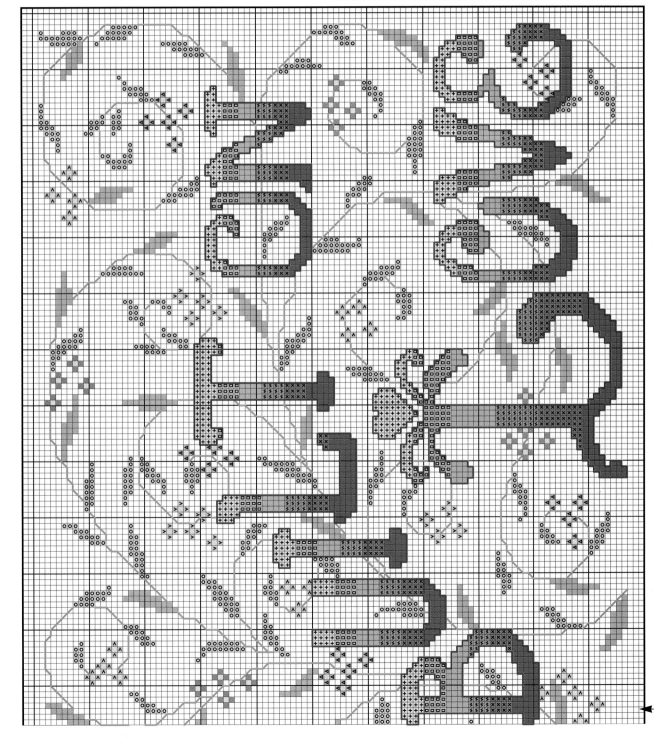

Blessed are the children
Who are Loved
And Know they are Loved
For they shall sow seeds of Love
Throughout the world
And reap joy for themselves
And for others.

Blessed are the Children
DESIGNED BY EVE ANDRADE

MATERIALS:

14" x 17" piece of white 14-count Aida

INSTRUCTIONS:

1. Center and stitch design, using two strands floss for Cross Stitch; use one strand floss for Cross Stitch of rainbow. Use two strands floss for Backstitch of lettering, birds in rainbow and shovel handles. Use one strand floss for remaining Backstitch.❖

Stitch Count:
102 wide x 134 high

Approximate Design Size:
11-count 9⅜" x 12¼"
14-count 7⅜" x 9⅝"
16-count 6⅜" x 8⅜"
18-count 5¾" x 7½"
22-count 4⅝" x 6⅛"

X	B'st	¼x	Fr	DMC	ANCHOR	J.&P. COATS	COLORS
				#211	#342	#4303	Lavender Lt.
				#309	#42	#3284	Rose Deep
				#334	#977	#7977	Baby Blue Med.
				#445	#288	#2288	Lemon Lt.
				#738	#372	#5375	Tan Ultra Lt.
			●	#783	#307	#2307	Christmas Gold
				#796	#133	#7100	Royal Blue Dk.
				#827	#159	#7159	Blue Very Lt.
				#842	#388	#5933	Beige Brown Ultra Very Lt.
				#869	#944	#5374	Brown Med.
				#899	#55	#3282	Rose Med.
				#938	#381	#5477	Coffee Brown Ultra Dk.
				#950	#4146	#2336	Terra Cotta Very Lt.
				#964	#185	#6185	Aquamarine Lt.
				#3326	#36	#3126	Melon Lt.
				#3716	#25	#3150	Dusty Rose Very Lt.

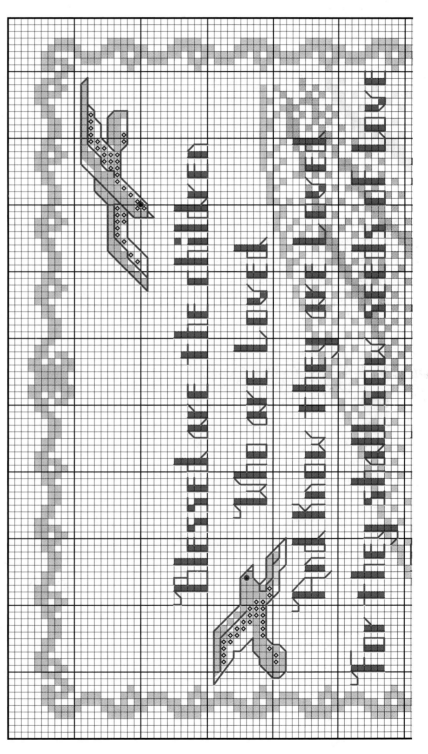

Graph continued on next page

X	B'st	1/4x	Fr	DMC	ANCHOR	J.&P. COATS	COLORS
				#211	#342	#4303	Lavender Lt.
				#309	#42	#3284	Rose Deep
				#334	#977	#7977	Baby Blue Med.
				#445	#288	#2288	Lemon Lt.
				#738	#372	#5375	Tan Ultra Lt.
				#783	#307	#2307	Christmas Gold
				#796	#133	#7100	Royal Blue Dk.
				#827	#159	#7159	Blue Very Lt.

X	B'st	1/4x	DMC	ANCHOR	J.&P. COATS	COLORS
			#842	#388	#5933	Beige Brown Ultra Very Lt.
			#869	#944	#5374	Brown Med.
			#899	#55	#3282	Rose Med.
			#938	#381	#5477	Coffee Brown Ultra Dk.
			#950	#4146	#2336	Terra Cotta Very Lt.
			#964	#185	#6185	Aquamarine Lt.
			#3326	#36	#3126	Melon Lt.
			#3716	#25	#3150	Dusty Rose Very Lt.

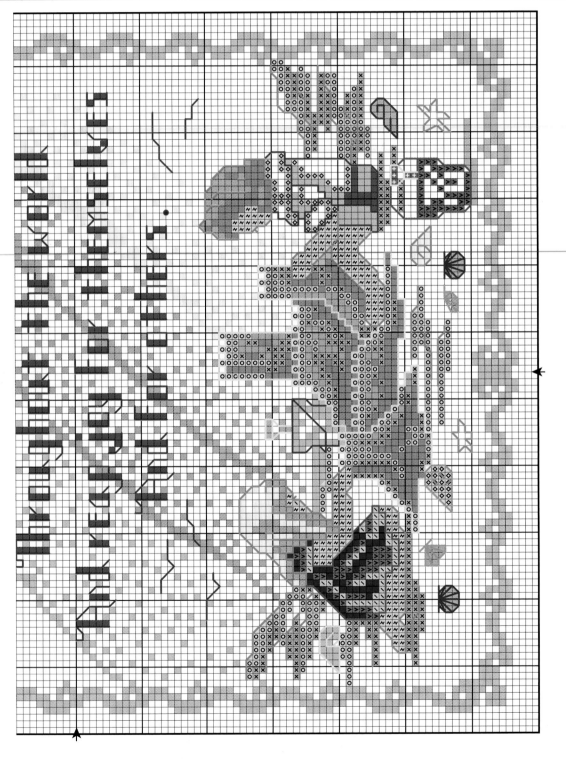

To My Mother

The cross-stitched sampler reads:

To My Mother

When I was little you were there
To wipe away my tears;
You applauded my successes
And calmed my midnight fears.
You showed me by example
The ways to happiness;
I honor you and love you Mom
You've given me the best.

Instructions on next page

To My Mother

DESIGNED BY VIRGINIA G. SOSKIN

MATERIALS:

13" x 15" piece of white 14-count Aida

INSTRUCTIONS:

1: Center and stitch design, using two strands floss or one strand floss held together with one strand blending filament for Cross Stitch. Use one strand floss for Backstitch and French Knots. Use one strand metallic braid for Running Stitch.❖

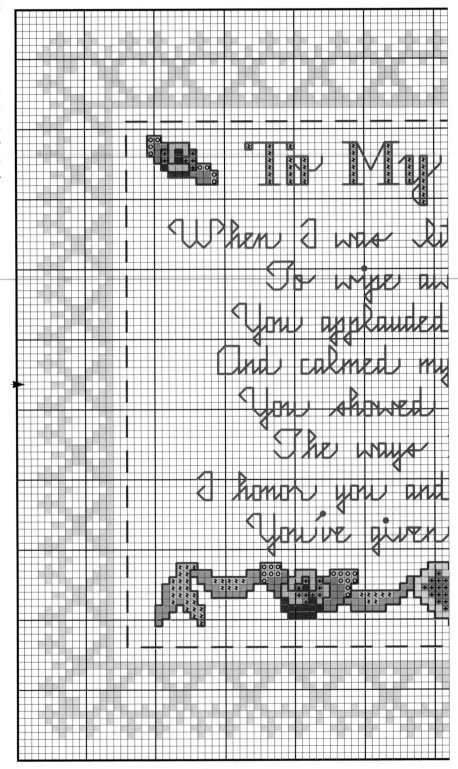

X	B'st	Run	Fr	DMC	ANCHOR	JPC	COLORS	KRIENIK (BF)	KRIENIK (MB)
■				#522	#860	#6316	Fern Green		
◙				#524	#858	#6315	Fern Green Very Lt.		
▦				#807	#168	#7168	Wedgewood Lt.		
	✎			#938	#381	#5477	Coffee Brown Ultra Dk.		
▨				#3047	#885	#2300	Yellow Beige Lt.	#002 Gold	
■				#3687	#68	#3088	Mauve		
✚				#3688	#60	#3087	Mauve Med.		
≥				#3689	#49	#3086	Mauve Lt.		
≷				#3766	#167	#7167	Sky Blue		
	✎		●	#3768	#779	#6876	Blue Green		
			✎						#007 Pink

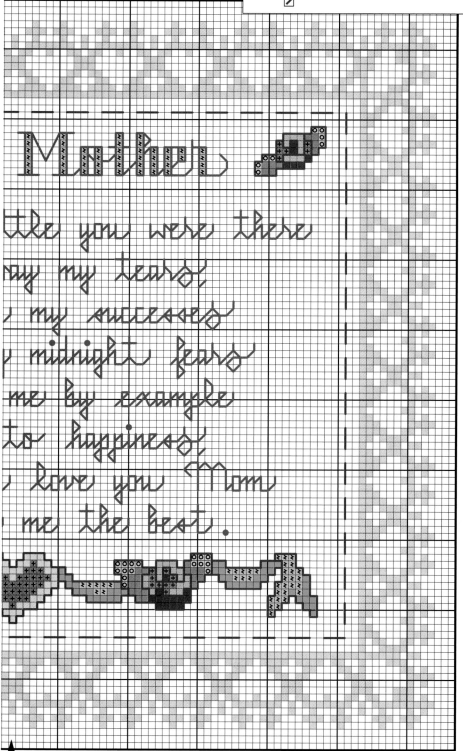

Stitch Count:
121 wide x 101 high

Approximate Design Size:
11-count 11" x 9¼"
14-count 8¾" x 7¼"
16-count 7⅝" x 6⅜"
18-count 6¾" x 5⅝"
22-count 5½" x 4⅝"

Victorian Grace

Harken back to a slower,
more peaceful time – an era
of genteel elegance, when
women of leisure spent
afternoons creating fine
lace and stitching
elaborate samplers ...
each perfect, ornate stitch
the measure of a woman's
skill with thread and needle
and a tribute to her
feminine artistry.

Victoriana

Victoriana
Battenberg lace and Balmoral heather,
Regatta races in breezy weather;
Roses, wicker and scrapbook collections;
Victorian things are life's confections.

Instructions on next page

Victoriana

DESIGNED BY VIRGINIA G. SOSKIN

MATERIALS:

14" x 15" piece of mushroom 14-count Aida

INSTRUCTIONS:

1. Center and stitch design, using one strand thread for Cross Stitch, Backstitch, Straight Stitch and French Knots. Use Ribbon Floss™ for Straight Stitch of border.❖

Stitch Count:
123 wide x 114 high

Approximate Design Size:
11-count 11¼" x 10⅜"
14-count 8⅞" x 8¼"
16-count 7¾" x 7⅛"
18-count 6⅞" x 6⅜"
22-count 5⅝" x 5¼"

X	B'st	Str	¼x	Fr	DMC (FT)	DMC	ANCHOR	J.&P. COATS	COLORS	RIBBON FLOSS™
▣					#2320	#320	#215	#6017	Pistachio Green Med.	
▦					#2358	#341	#117	#7005	Blue Violet Lt.	
✕					#2369	#369	#259	#6015	Pistachio Green Very Lt.	
▧					#2396	#554	#96	#4104	Lavender Dk.	
V					#2502	#502	#877	#6876	Blue Green	
◉		✎			#2597	#597	#168	#7168	Wedgewood Lt.	
▣					#2759	#754	#6	#2331	Peach Flesh Very Lt.	
▨					#2760	#760	#9	#3069	Salmon	
D					#2800	#800	#129	#7020	Delft Pale	
▲					#2818	#818	#23	#3281	Pink Med.	
▢		✎	▢		#2828	#828	#158	#7053	Larkspur Lt.	
⋀	✎			●	#2839	#839	#360	#5360	Beige Brown Very Dk.	
▨					#2841	#841	#378	#5376	Beige Brown Lt.	
＋					#2842	#842	#388	#5933	Beige Brown Ultra Very Lt.	
♡					White	White	#2	#1001	White	
▢					Ecru	Ecru	#387	#1002	Off White	
		✎								#20 Lt. Green

Victoriana

...enberg lace and Balmoral heather;
...gatta races in breezy weather;
..., wicker and scrapbook collections;
...rian things are life's confections.

Instructions on next page

Victorian Nosegays

Designed by Kathleen Hurley

MATERIALS:

Two 10" x 12" pieces of white 14-count Aida

INSTRUCTIONS:

1: Center and stitch one design

onto each piece of Aida, using two strands floss for Cross Stitch and one strand floss for Backstitch.❖

Hearts

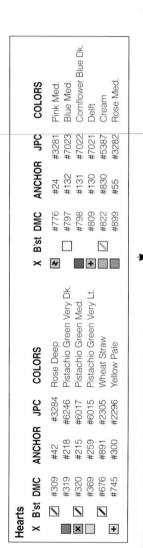

Hearts					
X	B'st	DMC	ANCHOR	JPC	COLORS
		#309	#42	#3284	Rose Deep
		#319	#218	#6246	Pistachio Green Very Dk.
		#320	#215	#6017	Pistachio Green Med.
		#369	#259	#6015	Pistachio Green Very Lt.
		#676	#891	#2305	Wheat Straw
		#745	#300	#2296	Yellow Pale

X	B'st	DMC	ANCHOR	JPC	COLORS
		#776	#24	#3281	Pink Med.
		#797	#132	#7023	Blue Med.
		#798	#131	#7022	Cornflower Blue Dk.
		#809	#130	#7021	Delft
		#822	#830	#5387	Cream
		#899	#55	#3282	Rose Med.

Stitch Count:
64 wide x 92 high

Approximate Design Size:
11-count 5⅞" x 8⅜"
14-count 4⅝" x 6⅝"
16-count 4" x 5¾"
18-count 3⅝" x 5⅛"
22-count 3" x 4¼"

Violets

X	B'st	DMC	ANCHOR	JPC	COLORS
■		#208	#110	#4301	Lavender Med.
■		#211	#342	#4303	Lavender Lt.
■		#319	#218	#6246	Pistachio Green Very Dk.
☒	╱	#320	#215	#6017	Pistachio Green Med.
	╱	#335	#38	#3283	Rose
□		#369	#259	#6015	Pistachio Green Very Lt.
■	╱	#550	#101	#4107	Violet Very Dk.
✛		#745	#300	#2296	Yellow Pale
☇		#776	#24	#3281	Pink Med.
■	╱	#822	#830	#5387	Cream
■		#899	#55	#3282	Rose Med.

Violets

Home Sweet Home

Designed by Kathleen Hurley

MATERIALS:

9" x 12" piece of brown 14-count perforated paper; Frame with 11" x 14" opening; 11" x 14" piece of black felt mat board; Antique treasures of choice; Craft glue or glue gun

INSTRUCTIONS:

1: Center and stitch design, using two strands floss for Cross Stitch and one strand floss for Backstitch. Trim stitched perforated paper following graph.

2: Center and glue trimmed design onto black felt mat board; glue board inside frame opening. Secure antique treasures around design as shown in photo. ❖

Stitch Count:
132 wide x 113 high

Approximate Design Size:
11-count 12" x 10⅜"
14-count 9½" x 8⅛"
16-count 8¼" x 7⅛"
18-count 7⅜" x 6⅜"
22-count 6" x 5⅛"

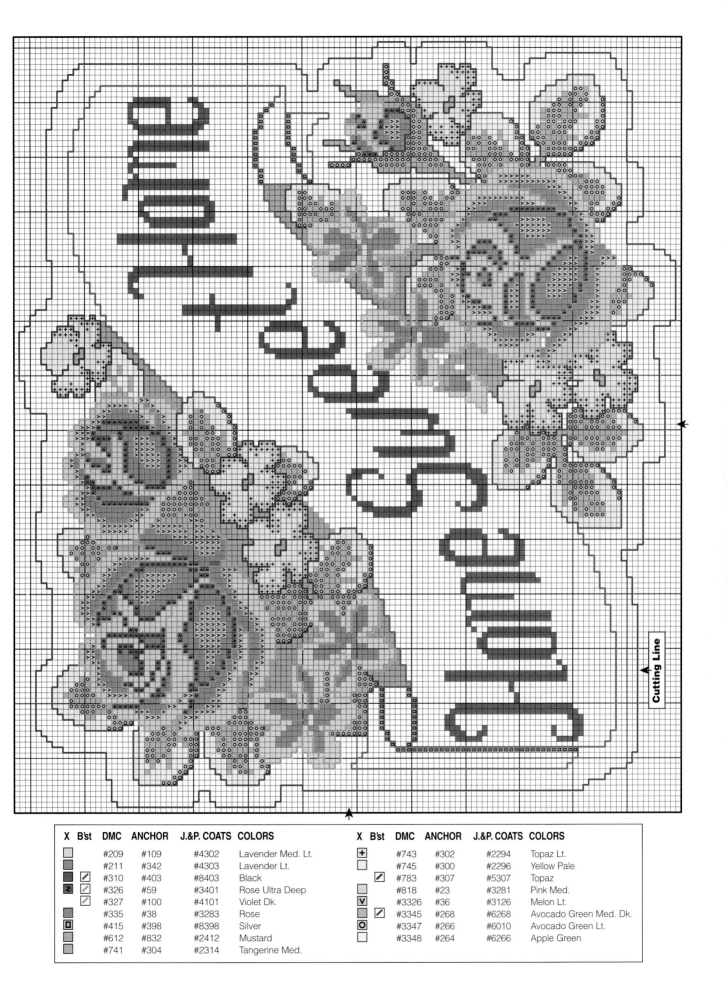

Cutting Line

X	B'st	DMC	ANCHOR	J.&P. COATS	COLORS	X	B'st	DMC	ANCHOR	J.&P. COATS	COLORS
		#209	#109	#4302	Lavender Med. Lt.	+		#743	#302	#2294	Topaz Lt.
		#211	#342	#4303	Lavender Lt.			#745	#300	#2296	Yellow Pale
	✎	#310	#403	#8403	Black		✎	#783	#307	#5307	Topaz
	✎	#326	#59	#3401	Rose Ultra Deep			#818	#23	#3281	Pink Med.
	✎	#327	#100	#4101	Violet Dk.	V		#3326	#36	#3126	Melon Lt.
		#335	#38	#3283	Rose		✎	#3345	#268	#6268	Avocado Green Med. Dk.
◘		#415	#398	#8398	Silver	O		#3347	#266	#6010	Avocado Green Lt.
		#612	#832	#2412	Mustard			#3348	#264	#6266	Apple Green
		#741	#304	#2314	Tangerine Med.						

VICTORIAN GRACE

A Thousand Flowers

DESIGNED BY JACQUELYN FOX

MATERIALS:

14" x 18" piece of periwinkle 28-count Pastel Linen; Frame with 11¼" x 14⅜" opening; Foam core board; Craft glue

INSTRUCTIONS:

NOTE: Double mat was professionally cut at a local frame shop.

1: Center and stitch design, stitching over two threads and using two strands floss for Cross Stitch. Use two strands floss for Backstitch and French Knots of lettering and rose stems. Use one strand floss for remaining Backstitch.❖

Stitch Count:
106 wide x 160 high

Approximate Design Size:
11-count 9⅝" x 14⅝"

14-count 7⅝" x 11½"
16-count 6⅝" x 10"
18-count 6" x 9"
22-count 4⅞" x 7⅜"
28-count over two threads
  7⅝" x 11½"

Color Key & Graph continued on next page

VICTORIAN GRACE

A Thousand Flowers

Instructions on page 32

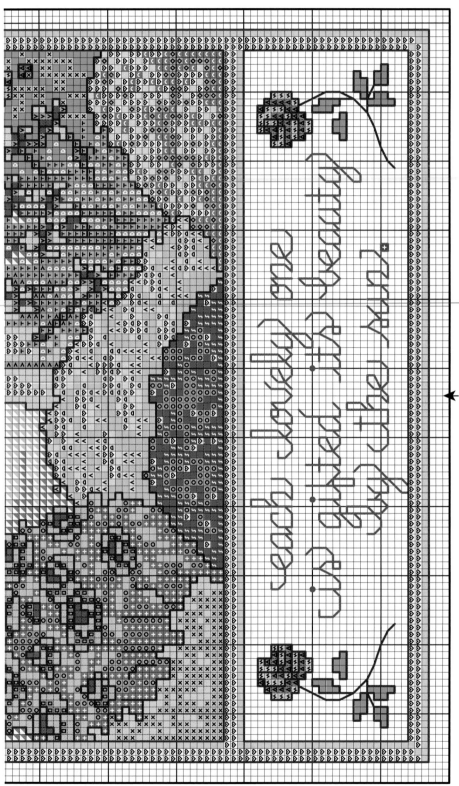

X	B'st	1/2x	3/4x	DMC	ANCHOR	J.&P. COATS	COLORS
				#899	#52	#3282	Rose Med.
				#911	#205	#6205	Emerald Green Med.
				#932	#1033	#7050	Antique Blue Lt.
				#937	#268	#6268	Avocado Green Med. Dk.
				#945	#881	#3335	Sportsman Flesh
				#954	#203	#6030	Nile Green Lt.
				#3046	#887	#2410	Mustard Lt.
				#3047	#852	#2300	Yellow Beige Lt.
				#3363	#262	#6316	Fern Green
				#3364	#260	#6266	Apple Green
				#3371	#382	#5382	Brown Grey Dk.
				#3687	#68	#3088	Mauve
				#3689	#49		Mauve Lt.
				White	#2	#1001	White

X	B'st	1/2x	1/4x	3/4x	Fr	DMC	ANCHOR	J.&P. COATS	COLORS
						#471	#266	#6266	Apple Green
						#472	#253	#6253	Avocado Green Ultra Lt.
						#500	#683	#6880	Blue Green Very Dk.
						#501	#878	#6878	Blue Green Dk.
						#503	#876	#6879	Blue Green Med.
						#676	#891	#2305	Wheat Straw
						#677	#886	#5372	Tan Lt.
						#739	#387	#5369	Tan Ultra Very Lt.
						#743	#302	#2294	Topaz Lt.
						#744	#301	#2293	Yellow Dark
						#746	#275	#2275	Lt. Cream
						#775	#128	#7031	Delft Very Pale
						#776	#24	#3281	Pink Med.
						#825	#162	#7181	Blue Dk.
						#890	#218	#6021	Pistachio Green Ultra Dk.

X	B'st	1/4x	3/4x	Fr	DMC	ANCHOR	J.&P. COATS	COLORS
					#208	#110	#4301	Lavender Med.
					#209	#109	#4302	Lavender Med. Lt.
					#210	#108	#4303	Lavender Lt.
					#309	#42	#3284	Rose Deep
					#312	#979	#7979	Navy Blue Lt.
					#319	#218	#6246	Pistachio Green Very Dk.
					#320	#215	#6017	Pistachio Green Med.
					#322	#978	#7978	Navy Blue Very Lt.
					#367	#217	#6018	Pistachio Green Dk.
					#415	#398	#8398	Silver
					#433	#358	#5471	Coffee Brown
					#435	#1046	#5371	Topaz Very Ultra Dk.
					#437	#362	#5942	Tan Brown Lt.
					#470	#267	#6010	Avocado Green Lt.

Cherubs & Hearts

Instructions on next page

Cherubs & Hearts

DESIGNED BY JACQUELYN FOX

MATERIALS:

One 13" x 14" piece, one 4" x 4" piece and one 6" x width of chipwood box lid piece of white 14-count Aida; 1¼ yds. soft white 14-count Gloria® 55" afghan fabric; 6" round chipwood box; Silver bow pendant with a 1¼" x 1⅝" oval frame; Frame with 10¾" x 11½" opening; Foam core board; Craft glue; ¼ yd. fabric or paint

INSTRUCTIONS:

NOTES: Double mat was professionally cut at a local frame shop. For afghan, chart rose motif onto graph paper to assure proper spacing as shown in photo. For chipwood box, chart border and hearts design onto graph paper to assure proper spacing.

1: For sampler, center and stitch design onto 13" x 14" piece of Aida, using two strands floss for Cross Stitch. Use two strands floss for French Knots, Lazy Daisy Stitch and for Backstitch of flower stems and vines. Use one strand floss for remaining Backstitch.

2: For afghan, center and stitch roses between border section of afghan fabric, stitching over two threads and using six strands floss for Cross Stitch and two strands floss for Backstitch. Fringe edges.

3: For chipwood box, center and stitch desired motif and border onto 6" x width of lid piece of Aida, using two strands floss for Cross Stitch and one strand floss for Backstitch. Cover box with fabric, or paint as desired. Trim stitched design slightly larger than lid lip. Press edges under; glue to lid lip as shown in photo.

4: For pendant, center and stitch one rose motif onto 4" x 4" piece of Aida, using two strands floss for Cross Stitch and one strand floss for Backstitch. Mount design into oval frame following manufacturer's instructions.❖

X	B'st	¼x	Fr	LzD	DMC	ANCHOR	J.&P. COATS	COLORS
D				●	#210	#108	#4303	Lavender Lt.
	□				#311	#148	#7980	Navy Blue Med.
■					#319	#218	#6246	Pistachio Green Very Dk.
⌇					#320	#215	#6017	Pistachio Green Med.
■					#334	#977	#7977	Baby Blue Med.
	╱			Ⓥ	#367	#217	#6018	Pistachio Green Dk.
■					#368	#214	#6016	Pistachio Green Lt.
	╱				#550	#102	#4107	Violet Very Dk.
■					#553	#98	#4097	Violet Lt.
▲					#554	#96	#4104	Lavender Dk.
□					#744	#301	#2293	Yellow Dk.
+		◺			#754	#1012	#2331	Peach Flesh Very Lt.
■					#758	#882	#2337	Terra Cotta Lt.
■					#760	#1022	#3069	Salmon

X	B'st	¼x	DMC	ANCHOR	J.&P. COATS	COLORS
✕			#761	#1021	#3068	Salmon Lt.
⋈			#775	#128	#7031	Delft Very Pale
⑀			#839	#360	#5360	Beige Brown Very Dk.
■			#841	#378	#5376	Beige Brown Lt.
	╱		#890	#218	#6021	Pistachio Green Ultra Dk.
	╱		#938	#381	#5381	Mocha Brown Very Dk.
□		□	#948	#1011	#3239	Shell Pink Lt.
◇	╱		#3350	#59	#3004	Dusty Rose Very Dk.
■			#3354	#74	#3003	Dusty Rose Lt.
		◣	#3371	#382	#5382	Brown Grey Dk.
V			#3713	#1020	#3068	Salmon Lt.
Λ			#3731	#76	#3176	Antique Rose Med.
Ⓞ			#3755	#140	#7976	Baby Blue

Stitch Count:
101 wide x 112 high

**Approximate
Design Size:**
11-count 9¼" x 10¼"
14-count 7¼" x 8"
16-count 6⅜" x 7"
18-count 5⅝" x 6¼"
22-count 4⅝" x 5⅛"

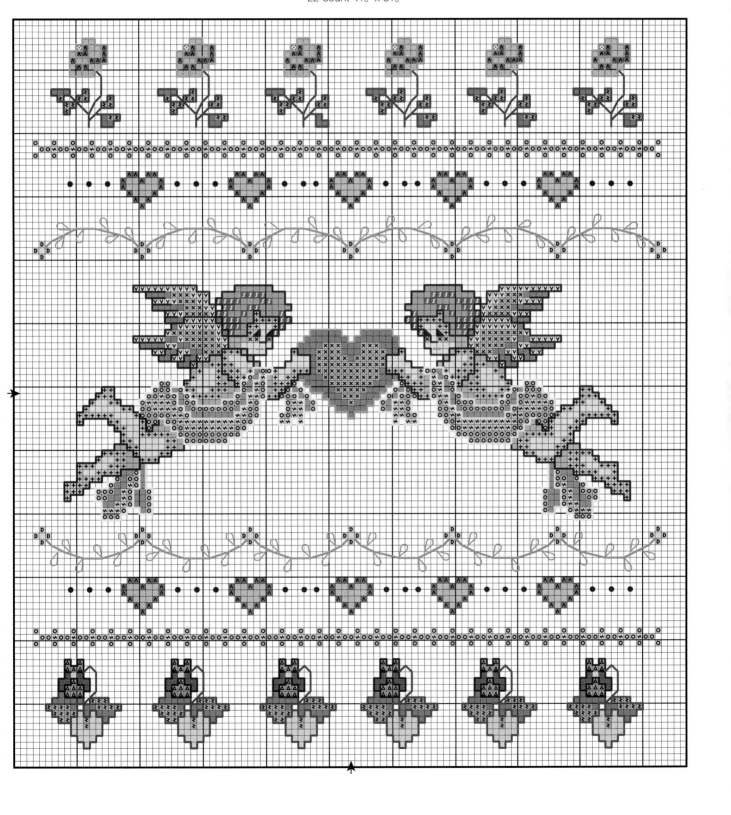

Victorian Afghan

DESIGNED BY C.M. BARR

MATERIALS:
50" x 59" piece of white 14-count afghan fabric; 7½ yds. lt. blue ½" satin ribbon with picot edge

INSTRUCTIONS:
NOTE: Cut ribbon into fifteen 18" lengths and tie into bows.

1: Stitch one design on each square following Placement Diagram on page 40, using two strands floss for Cross Stitch and Backstitch. Sew one bow on each empty square.

2: To fringe afghan, pull and remove one fabric thread 3½" from outside edge; unravel all threads from fabric edge to missing thread.❖

Heart

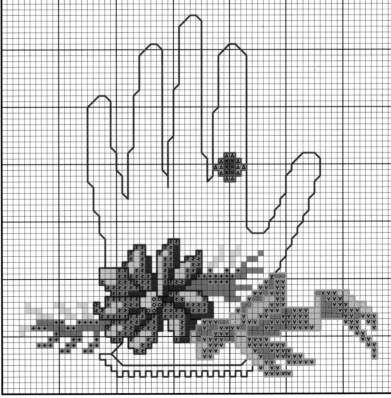

**Heart, Fan & Glove
Stitch Count:**
63 wide x 63 high

**Approximate
Design Size:**
11-count 5¾" x 5¾"
14-count 4½" x 4½"
16-count 4" x 4"
18-count 3½" x 3½"
22-count 2⅞" x 2⅞"

Heart

X	B'st	DMC	ANCHOR	JPC	COLORS	X	B'st	DMC	ANCHOR	JPC	COLORS
■	✎	#500	#879	#6880	Blue Green Very Dk.	■		#3687	#68	#3088	Mauve
V		#502	#877	#6876	Blue Green	≥		#3688	#60	#3087	Mauve Med.
☐		#504	#213	#6875	Blue Green Lt.	☐		#3689	#49	#3086	Mauve Lt.
▨		#930	#922	#7052	Antique Blue Dk.	☐	✎	#3750	#922	#7980	Navy Blue Med.
+		#931	#921	#7051	Antique Blue Med.	☐		#3752	#976	#7050	Antique Blue Lt.
◎	✎	#3685	#70	#3089	Mauve Dk.						

Glove

Glove

X	B'st	DMC	ANCHOR	JPC	COLORS
■		#311	#148	#7980	Navy Blue Med.
	✎	#315	#972	#3243	Shell Pink Dk.
V		#316	#969	#3081	Antique Mauve Med.
≥		#322	#978	#7978	Navy Blue Very Lt.
+		#469	#267	#6261	Avocado Green Med.
☐		#471	#265	#6010	Avocado Green Lt.
☐		#725	#305	#2298	Canary Deep
☐		#778	#969	#3080	Antique Mauve Lt.
	✎	#780	#365	#5000	Russet
◎		#782	#308	#5365	Brown Very Lt.
△		#783	#307	#2307	Christmas Gold
	✎	#823	#127	#7982	Navy Blue Very Dk.
▨		#934	#862	#6270	Black Avocado Green
☐		#3325	#144	#7976	Baby Blue
▨		#3726	#970	#3082	Antique Mauve Dk.
✕		#3746	#119	#7150	Cornflower Blue Very Dk.

Graphs continued on next page

Fan

X	B'st	DMC	ANCHOR	JPC	COLORS
■	✎	#500	#879	#6880	Blue Green Very Dk.
V		#502	#877	#6876	Blue Green
▫		#504	#213	#6875	Blue Green Lt.
▨		#930	#922	#7052	Antique Blue Dk.
+		#931	#921	#7051	Antique Blue Med.
◪	✎	#3685	#70	#3089	Mauve Dk.

X	B'st	DMC	ANCHOR	JPC	COLORS
■		#3687	#68	#3088	Mauve
≈		#3688	#60	#3087	Mauve Med.
▫		#3689	#49	#3086	Mauve Lt.
	✎	#3750	#922	#7980	Navy Blue Med.
▨		#3752	#976	#7050	Antique Blue Lt.

Fan

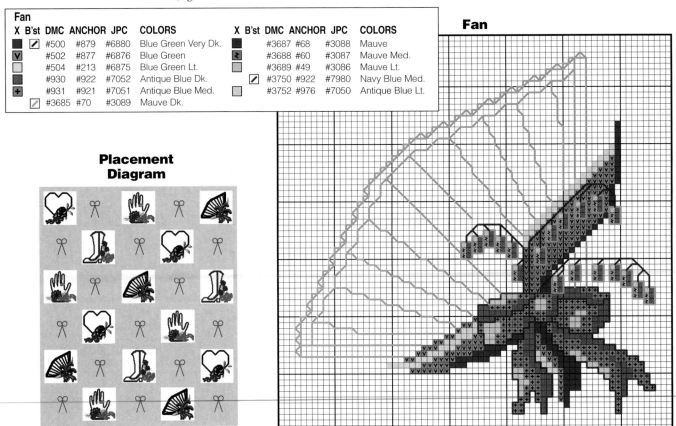

Placement Diagram

Shoe

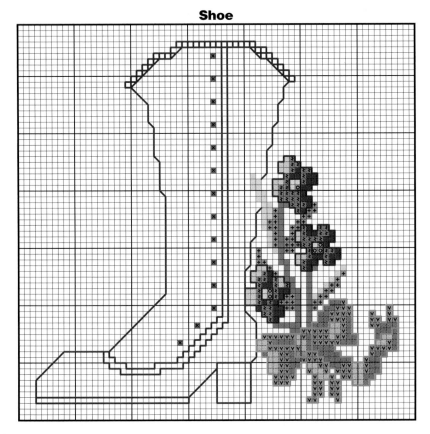

Shoe

Stitch Count:
64 wide x 63 high

Approximate Design Size:
11-count 5⅞" x 5¾"
14-count 4⅝" x 4½"
16-count 4" x 4"
18-count 3⅝" x 3½"
22-count 3" x 2⅞"

Shoe

X	B'st	DMC	ANCHOR	JPC	COLORS
■		#311	#148	#7980	Navy Blue Med.
	✎	#315	#972	#3243	Shell Pink Dk.
V		#316	#969	#3081	Antique Mauve Med.
≈		#322	#978	#7978	Navy Blue Very Lt.
+		#469	#267	#6261	Avocado Green Med.
▫		#471	#265	#6010	Avocado Green Lt.
▫		#725	#305	#2298	Canary Deep
▫		#778	#969	#3080	Antique Mauve Lt.
	✎	#780	#365	#5000	Russet
O		#782	#308	#5365	Brown Very Lt.
△		#783	#307	#2307	Christmas Gold
	✎	#823	#127	#7982	Navy Blue Very Dk.
▨		#934	#862	#6270	Black Avocado Green
▫		#3325	#144	#7976	Baby Blue
▨		#3726	#970	#3082	Antique Mauve Dk.
✕		#3746	#119	#7150	Cornflower Blue Very Dk.

Sampler Charm

Recreate a cross stitched
masterpiece from this varied
collection of samplers.
Originally the true test of a
woman's needlework skills,
the sampler became a canvas
on which dreams and
histories were recorded
and preserved ...
each stitch an expression
of a stitcher's style
and creativity.

Flowers for My Lady

DESIGNED BY
JUDY CHRISPENS

MATERIALS:

14" x 18" piece of ivory 28-count Annabelle; Frame with 12¾" x 16⅝" opening; Foam core board; Craft glue or glue gun

INSTRUCTIONS:

NOTE: Double mat was professionally cut at a local frame shop.

1: Center and stitch design, stitching over two threads and using two strands floss for Cross Stitch and one strand floss for Backstitch.❖

Graph continued on next page

Flowers for My Lady

Graph continued from page 43

Stitch Count:
172 wide x 117 high

Approximate Design Size:
11-count 15⅝" x 10⅝"

14-count 12⅜" x 8⅜"
16-count 10¾" x 7⅜"
18-count 9⅝" x 6½"
22-count 7⅞" x 5⅜"
28-count over two threads 12⅜" x 8⅜"

X	B'st	¼x	Fr	DMC	ANCHOR	J.&P. COATS	COLORS
				#612	#853	#2412	Mustard
				#730	#924	#6261	Avocado Green Med.
				#732	#281	#6010	Avocado Green Lt.
				#819	#271	#3280	Baby Pink Lt.
			●	#930	#922	#7052	Antique Blue Dk.
				#932	#920	#7050	Antique Blue Lt.
				#3012	#843	#6253	Avocado Green Ultra Lt.
				#3051	#846	#6317	Pine Green Med.
				#3713	#968	#3068	Salmon Lt.
				#3722	#896	#3241	Shell Pink Med.
				#3727	#969	#3081	Antique Mauve Med.

ned by tina zednick

Cottage Sampler

DESIGNED BY JUDY CHRISPENS

MATERIALS:

13" x 17" piece of ivory 14-count Aida; Wooden frame with 11½" x 15" opening; Foam core board; Craft glue or glue gun

INSTRUCTIONS:

NOTE: Mat was professionally cut at a local frame shop.

1: Center and stitch design, using two strands floss for Cross Stitch and one strand floss for Backstitch and French Knots.❖

Graph on next page

Cottage Sampler

Stitch Count:
102 wide x 155 high

Approximate Design Size:
11-count 9⅜" x 14⅛"
14-count 7⅜" x 11⅛"
16-count 6⅜" x 9¾"
18-count 5¾" x 8⅝"
22-count 4⅝" x 7⅛"

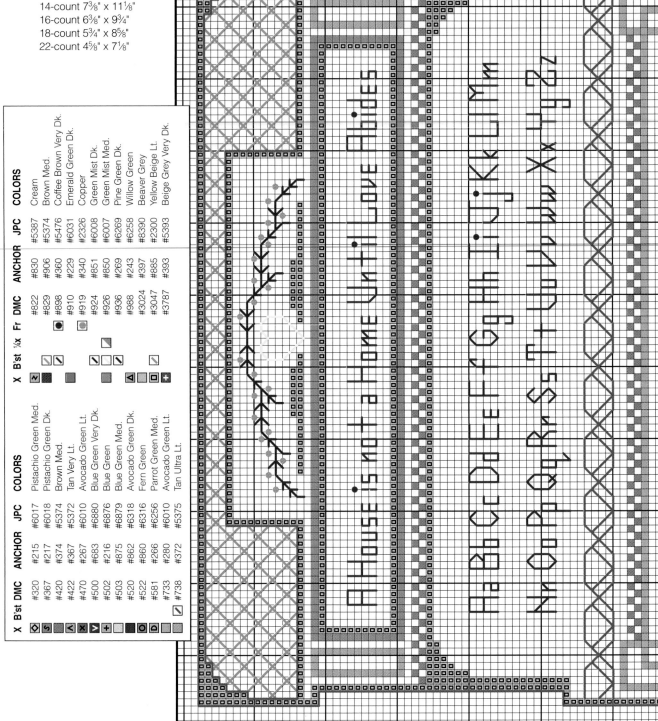

X	B'st	¼x	Fr	DMC	ANCHOR	JPC	COLORS
				#822	#830	#5387	Cream
				#829	#906	#5374	Brown Med.
				#898	#360	#5476	Coffee Brown Very Dk.
			●	#910	#229	#6031	Emerald Green Dk.
			●	#919	#340	#2326	Copper
				#924	#851	#6008	Green Mist Dk.
				#926	#850	#6007	Green Mist Med.
				#936	#269	#6269	Pine Green Dk.
				#988	#243	#6258	Willow Green
				#3024	#397	#8390	Beaver Grey
				#3047	#885	#2300	Yellow Beige Lt.
				#3787	#393	#5393	Beige Grey Very Dk.

X	B'st	DMC	ANCHOR	JPC	COLORS
		#320	#215	#6017	Pistachio Green Med.
		#367	#217	#6018	Pistachio Green Dk.
		#420	#374	#5374	Brown Med.
		#422	#367	#5372	Tan Very Lt.
		#470	#267	#6010	Avocado Green Lt.
		#500	#683	#6880	Blue Green Very Dk.
		#502	#216	#6876	Blue Green
		#503	#875	#6879	Blue Green Med.
		#520	#862	#6318	Avocado Green Dk.
		#522	#860	#6316	Fern Green
		#581	#266	#6256	Parrot Green Med.
		#733	#280	#6010	Avocado Green Lt.
		#738	#372	#5375	Tan Ultra Lt.

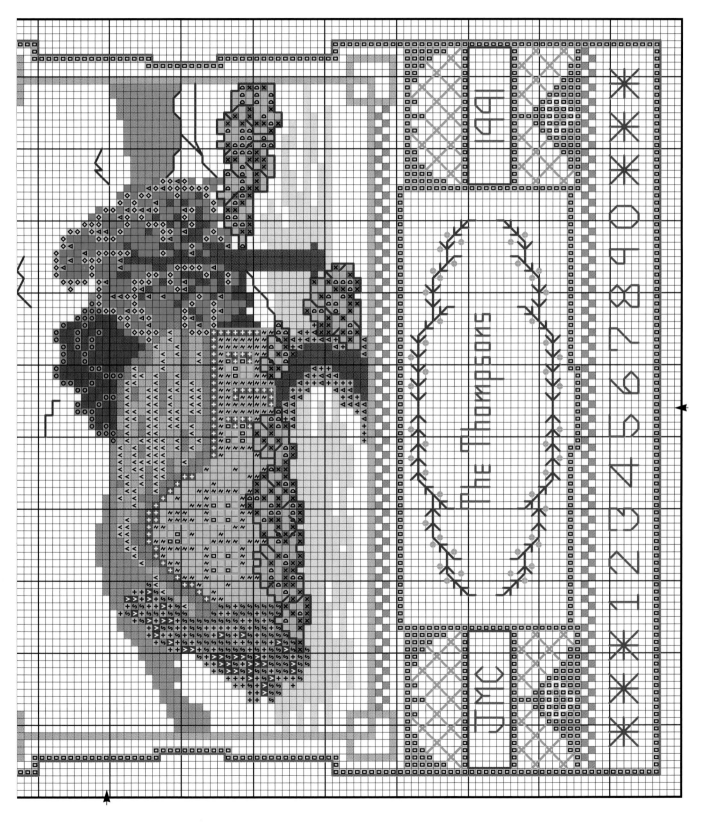

Love is the Answer

DESIGNED BY EVE ANDRADE

MATERIALS:

15" x 18" piece of cameo rose 14-count Aida

INSTRUCTIONS:

1: Center and stitch design, using two strands floss for Cross Stitch, Backstitch of lettering and French Knots. Use one strand floss for remaining Backstitch.❖

Graph on page 50

Stitch Count:
105 wide x 135 high

Approximate Design Size:
11-count 9⅝" x 12⅜"
14-count 7½" x 9¾"
16-count 6⅝" x 8½"
18-count 5⅞" x 7½"
22-count 4⅞" x 6⅛"

X	B'st	¼x	Fr	DMC	ANCHOR	J.&P. COATS	COLORS
	✔			#501	#878	#6878	Blue Green Dk.
▢	✔	▢		#502	#877	#6876	Blue Green
▨	✔		●	#924	#851	#6008	Green Mist Dk.
▢				#948	#778	#2331	Peach Flesh Very Lt.
		▢		#3046	#887	#2410	Mustard Lt.
◉		▢		#3326	#36	#3126	Melon Lt.
	✔		●	#3350	#59	#3004	Dusty Rose Very Dk.
■				#3731	#77	#3283	Rose

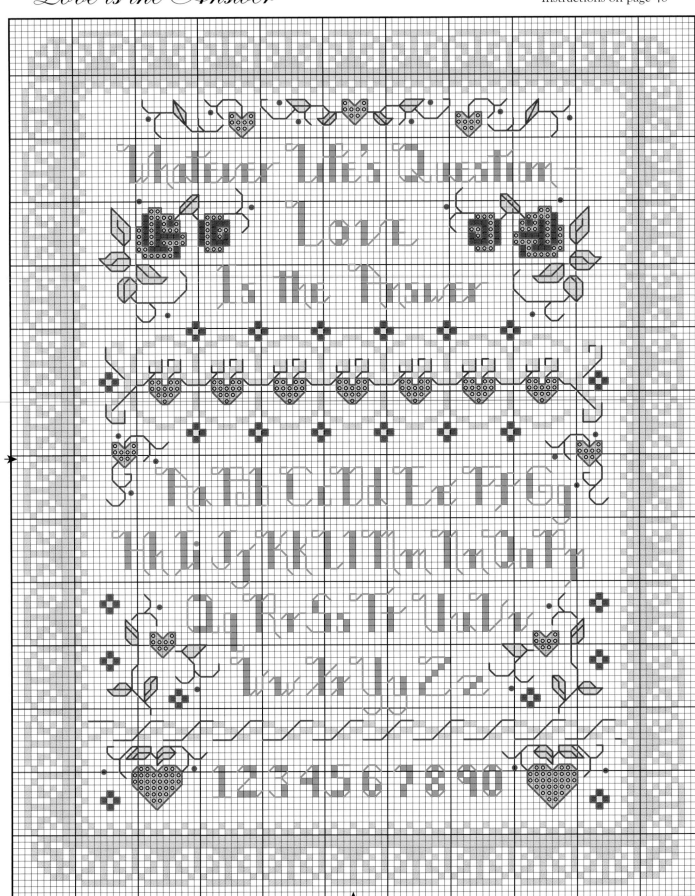

Sweet hearts pause in garden bower

A B C D E F G H
I J K L M N O P
Q R S T U V W
X Y Z

Lost in love between fern and flower

Instructions on next page

Fern & Flower

Designed by Virginia G. Soskin

MATERIALS:

One 12" x 15" and one 6" x 6" piece of white 14-count Aida; 4" x 5" oval applique; Pink porcelain box with 2⅝" design area

INSTRUCTIONS:

1: Center and stitch Sampler design onto 12" x 15" piece of Aida, Flowers design onto 6" x 6" piece of Aida and letters of choice onto applique, using two strands floss for Cross Stitch and one strand floss for Backstitch and French Knots.

2: Position and secure Flowers design into porcelain box following manufacturer's instructions. ❖

X	B'st	¼x	¾x	Fr	DMC	ANCHOR	JPC	COLORS
▲					#209	#109	#4302	Lavender Med. Lt.
⇄					#210	#108	#4303	Lavender Lt.
	✎				#320	#215	#6017	Pistachio Green Med.
■	✎				#340	#118	#7110	Blue Violet Med.
▨	✎				#341	#117	#7005	Blue Violet Lt.
▨	✎				#469	#267	#6261	Avocado Green Med.
▼	✎			●	#553	#98	#4097	Violet Lt.
☐		☐		☐	#743	#302	#2302	Orange Lt.
	✎				#987	#244	#6258	Willow Green
▨					#3347	#266	#6266	Apple Green
◖					#3607	#87	#3088	Mauve
➕					#3609	#85	#3087	Mauve Med.
▨					#3689	#49	#3086	Mauve Lt.
■	✎				#3746	#119	#7150	Cornflower Blue Very Dk.
	✎				#3787	#393	#5393	Beige Grey Very Dk.
♥			◨		White	#2	#1001	White

Flowers
Stitch Count:
23 wide x 20 high

Approximate
Design Size:
11-count 2⅛" x 1⅞"
14-count 1¾" x 1½"
16-count 1½" x 1¼"
18-count 1⅜" x 1⅛"
22-count 1⅛" x 1"

Sampler
Stitch Count:
125 wide x 90 high

Approximate
Design Size:
11-count 11⅜" x 8¼"
14-count 9" x 6½"
16-count 7⅞" x 5⅝"
18-count 7" x 5"
22-count 5¾" x 4⅛"

Flowers

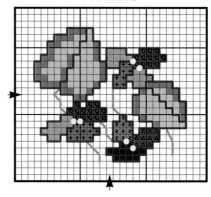

Sweethearts pause in garden bower

Lost in love between fern and flower

Jacobean Sampler

DESIGNED BY JUDY CHRISPENS

MATERIALS:

14" x 18" piece of tea-dyed 28-count Irish linen; Frame with 11½" x 15" opening; Foam core board; Craft glue or glue gun

INSTRUCTIONS:

NOTE: Mat was professionally cut at a local frame shop.

1: Choosing letters and numbers of choice from Alphabet & Numbers graph, center and stitch design, stitching over two threads and using two strands floss for Cross Stitch, Satin

Continued on page 56

Alphabet & Numbers

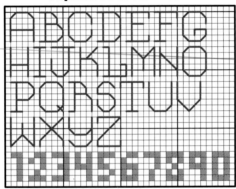

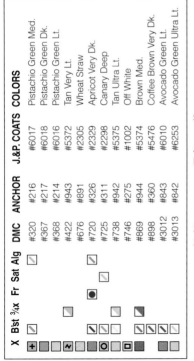

X	Bst	¾x	Fr	Sat	Alg	DMC	ANCHOR	J.&P. COATS	COLORS
						#320	#216	#6017	Pistachio Green Med.
						#367	#217	#6018	Pistachio Green Dk.
						#368	#214	#6016	Pistachio Green Lt.
						#422	#943	#5372	Tan Very Lt.
						#676	#891	#2305	Wheat Straw
						#720	#326	#2329	Apricot Very Dk.
						#725	#311	#2298	Canary Deep
						#738	#942	#5375	Tan Ultra Lt.
						#746	#275	#1002	Off White
						#869	#944	#5374	Brown Med.
						#898	#360	#5476	Coffee Brown Very Dk.
						#3012	#843	#6010	Avocado Green Lt.
						#3013	#842	#6253	Avocado Green Ultra Lt.

Stitch Count:
117 wide x 169 high

Approximate Design Size:
11-count 10⅝" x 15⅜"
14-count 8⅜" x 12⅛"
16-count 7⅜" x 10⅝"
18-count 6½" x 9⅜"
22-count 5⅜" x 7¾"
28-count over two
   threads 8⅜" x 12⅛"

Jacobean Sampler

Continued from page 54

Stitch, Algerian Eye and French Knots. Use two strands floss for Backstitch of vines, flower foliage, bird's plumes and feet, initials and box around "Wrought With Heart And Hand." Use one strand floss for remaining Backstitch. ❖

Algerian Eyelet Stitch Illustration

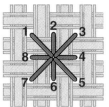

Border
Elegance

Display your favorite motifs
on trims and finished borders.
Once a way of preserving
collections of stitches, today
borders are stitched to
enhance frilly linens, dress up
a basket or tote bag or accent
a special shelf ...
each stitch adding the
perfect finishing touch to a
thoughtful gift or home
decor project.

Fragrant Borders

DESIGNED BY JACQUELYN FOX

MATERIALS:

Two ecru fingertip towels with a 2½" wide 14-count Aida border; Two ecru hang towels with a 3" wide 14-count Aida border

INSTRUCTIONS:

1: Center and stitch Lavender and Chamomile designs onto each fingertip towel, and Dill and Basil designs onto each hang towel, using two strands floss for Cross Stitch, Backstitch of lettering and stems and French Knots. Use one strand floss for remaining Backstitch.❖

Chamomile						
X	B'st	Fr	DMC	ANCHOR	J.&P. COATS	COLORS
	✓		#221	#897	#3243	Shell Pink Dk.
▨			#223	#895	#3240	Shell Pink
✓			#224	#893	#3239	Shell Pink Lt.
▨			#225	#1026	#3066	Coral Lt.
	✓		#500	#683	#6880	Blue Green Very Dk.
▨	✓	●	#501	#878	#6878	Blue Green Dk.
≷			#502	#877	#6876	Blue Green
▨			#676	#891	#2305	Wheat Straw
▨			#927	#848	#6006	Green Mist Lt.
✚			#3721	#896	#3242	Shell Pink Med. Dk.
◯			White	#2	#1001	White

Chamomile

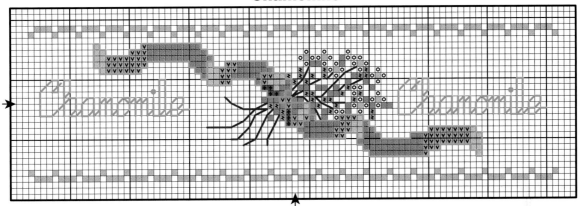

Dill						
X	B'st	Fr	DMC	ANCHOR	J.&P. COATS	COLORS
▨			#676	#891	#2305	Wheat Straw
▨			#677	#886	#5372	Tan Very Lt.
▨			#680	#901	#2876	Old Gold Dk.
		●	#725	#305	#2294	Topaz Lt.
𝖲			#729	#890	#2875	Wheat Straw Dk.
	✓		#895	#1044	#6021	Pistachio Green Ultra Dk.
	✓		#938	#381	#5381	Mocha Brown Very Dk.
▨	✓		#3346	#267	#6261	Avocado Green Med.

Stitch Count:
89 wide x 26 high

Approximate Design Size:
11-count 8⅛" x 2⅜"
14-count 6⅜" x 1⅞"
16-count 5⅝" x 1⅝"
18-count 5" x 1½"
22-count 4⅛" x 1¼"

Dill

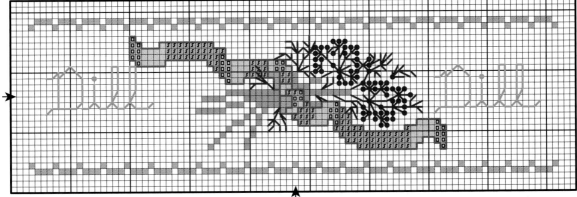

Graphs continued on next page

Lavender				
X	B'st	DMC	ANCHOR	J.&P. COATS	COLORS
		#224	#893	#3239	Shell Pink Lt.
	✓	#501	#878	#6878	Blue Green Dk.
		#502	#877	#6876	Blue Green
	✓	#823	#152	#7982	Navy Blue Very Dk.
		#924	#851	#6008	Green Mist Dk.
		#927	#848	#6006	Green Mist Lt.
		#928	#274	#6005	Green Mist Very Lt.
		#3041	#871	#4222	Antique Violet
		#3042	#870	#4221	Antique Violet Lt.
	✓	#3740	#872	#4223	Antique Violet Med.
		#3768	#779	#6007	Green Mist Med.

Lavender

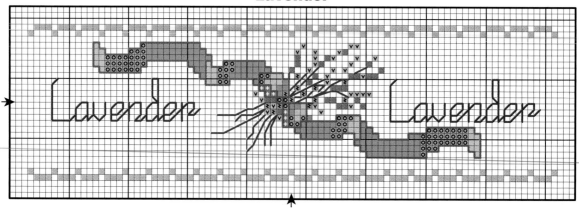

Basil					
X	B'st	Fr	DMC	ANCHOR	J.&P. COATS	COLORS
			#210	#108	#4303	Lavender Lt.
	✓		#791	#178	#7024	Royal Blue Very Dk.
			#792	#941	#7150	Cornflower Blue Very Dk.
			#793	#176	#7110	Blue Violet Med.
			#794	#175	#7977	Baby Blue Med.
	✓	●	#895	#1044	#6021	Pistachio Green Ultra Dk.
	✓		#3346	#267	#6261	Avocado Green Med.
			#3348	#264	#6266	Apple Green
			#3753	#1031	#7031	Delft Very Pale

Basil

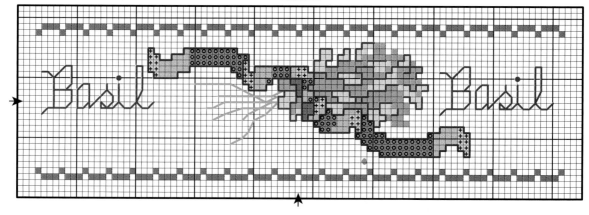

Swan Bath Set

Instructions on next page

61

Swan Bath Set

DESIGNED BY KATHLEEN MARIE O'DONNELL

MATERIALS:

One 6" x 21" piece and two 7" x 7" pieces of Williamsburg blue 18-count Aida; Blue hand towel; ½ yd. ecru 2¼" pre-gathered lace; 1 yd. ecru ¼" lace edging; ¼ yd white ¼" pre-gathered lace; ⅜" white ¼" satin ribbon; 3" round blue porcelain box; Small hand mirror; 2¾" round frame; Craft glue or glue gun

INSTRUCTIONS:

Towel

1: Center and stitch Towel design onto 6" x 21" piece of Aida, using two strands floss for Cross Stitch and one strand floss for Backstitch. Trim and press under all unfinished edges so piece measures width of towel and 2½" wide.

2: To construct towel, finish short edges of 2¼" pre-gathered lace to fit width of towel. Whipstitch lace to one short edge of towel 2¼" from lower edge.

3: Whipstitch stitched Aida onto towel, being sure to cover straight edge of lace. Hand sew lace edging over both long edges of stitched Aida.

Porcelain Box

1: Center and stitch Porcelain Box design onto 7" x 7" piece of Aida, using two strands floss for Cross Stitch and one strand floss for Backstitch. Trim and insert stitched piece into lid according to manufacturer's instructions.

Mirror

1: Center and stitch swan of choice from Towel design onto 7" x 7" piece of Aida, using two strands floss for Cross Stitch and one strand floss for Backstitch.

2: Trim and insert stitched piece into 2¾" frame. Glue ¼" pre-gathered lace around outside bottom edge of frame. Center and glue frame to back of mirror. Tie ribbon in bow; glue to mirror as shown in photo.❖

Towel
Stitch Count:
141 wide x 32 high

Approximate
Design Size:
11-count 12⅞" x 3"
14-count 10⅛" x 2⅜"
16-count 8⅞" x 2"
18-count 7⅞" x 1⅞"
22-count 6½" x 1½"

Towel

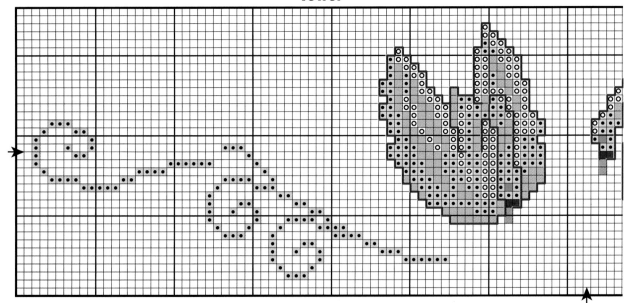

X	B'st	DMC	ANCHOR	J.&P. COATS	COLORS
■		#310	#403	#8403	Black
■		#336	#150	#7978	Navy Blue
■		#437	#362	#5942	Tan Brown Lt.
	✎	#642	#832	#5393	Beige Grey Very Dk.
	✎	#930	#922	#7052	Antique Blue Dk.
■		#3033	#391	#5388	Beige
•		Ecru	#387	#1002	Off White
○		White	#2	#1001	White

Porcelain Box

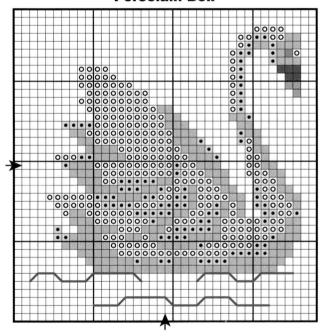

Porcelain Box Stitch Count:
34 wide x 35 high

Approximate Design Size:
11-count 3⅛" x 3¼"
14-count 2½" x 2½"
16-count 2⅛" x 2¼"
18-count 1⅞" x 2"
22-count 1⅝" x 1⅝"

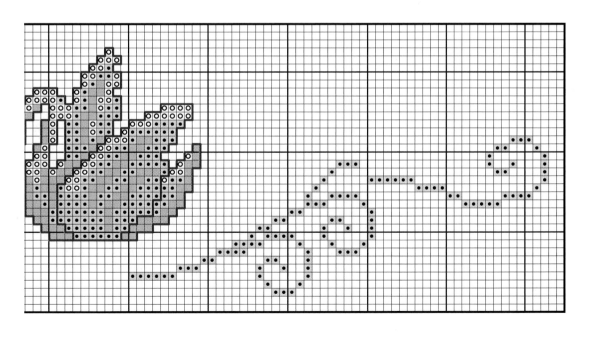

Formal Edging

DESIGNED BY JUDY CHRISPENS

MATERIALS:

One 17" x 28" piece and one 17" x 30½" piece of white 14-count Aida; ⅞ yd. white 45" fabric; 1 yd. white 2½" flat lace; Two 12" x 16" pillow forms

INSTRUCTIONS:

1: For straight edge pillow sham, center and stitch design onto 17" x 28" piece of Soft Touch Aida, placing bottom of design ½" from one 17" edge and continuing border design across, using two strands floss for Cross Stitch and one strand floss for Backstitch.

2: For "V" edge pillow sham, center and stitch flower motif only onto 17" x 30½" piece of Soft Touch Aida, placing bottom of design 2" from one 17" edge and using two strands floss for Cross Stitch and one strand floss for Backstitch.

NOTE: From fabric, cut one 17" x 28" piece and one 17" x 30½" piece for linings. From flat lace, cut one 17" length and one 19" length.

3: For straight edge pillow sham, with right sides together and with ½" seam, stitch 17" length of flat lace along stitched edge of Aida. Place lining on top; stitch both 17" edges. Trim seams; turn right side out; press.

4: With right sides together and with ½" seams, fold stitched 17" edge down 7½" and remaining 17" edge up 9", stitch side seams through all thicknesses. Trim seams and turn right side out. Insert pillow form.

5: For "V" edge pillow sham, trim stitched Soft Touch Aida and lining into "V" shape. Repeat steps #3 and #4, using 19" piece of lace.❖

Graph on next page

**Flower Motif
Stitch Count:**
81 wide × 58 high

**Approximate
Design Size:**
11-count 7⅜" × 5⅜"
14-count 5⅞" × 4¼"
16-count 5⅛" × 3⅝"
18-count 4½" × 3¼"
22-count 3¾" × 2⅝"

X	B'st	DMC	ANCHOR	J.&P. COATS	COLORS
		#3354	#74	#3003	Dusty Rose Lt.
		#3363	#262	#6317	Pine Green Med.
		#3364	#261	#6010	Avocado Green Lt.
		#3731	#77	#3283	Rose
		#3733	#75	#3282	Rose Med.
		#3752	#976	#7050	Antique Blue Lt.

X	B'st	DMC	ANCHOR	J.&P. COATS	COLORS
		#369	#259	#6015	Pistachio Green Very Lt.
		#420	#374	#5374	Brown Med.
		#437	#362	#5942	Tan Brown Lt.
		#738	#361	#5375	Tan Ultra Lt.
		#746	#275	#1002	Off White
		#775	#975	#7031	Delft Very Pale
		#963	#73	#3280	Baby Pink Lt.

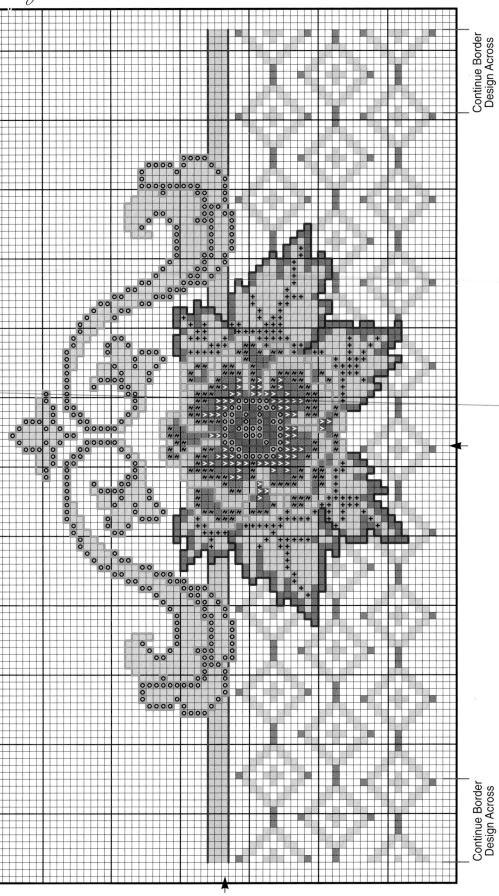

Continue Border
Design Across

Continue Border
Design Across

Lacy Hand Towels

Instructions on next page

Lacy Hand Towels

Designed by Kathleen Hurley

MATERIALS:

Three blue velour guest towels with cotton lace and 14-count Aida trim

INSTRUCTIONS:

1: Center and stitch one design onto each towel, using two strands floss for Cross Stitch and French Knots. Use one strand floss for Backstitch and Lazy Daisy Stitch.❖

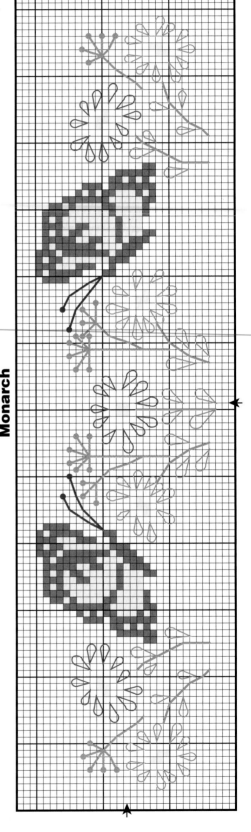

Monarch

Monarch				DMC	ANCHOR	J&P. COATS	COLORS
X	Bst	Fr	LzD				
●				#310	#403	#8403	Black
	⊘			#701	#227	#6226	Kelly Green
	⊘		⊘	#783	#307	#5307	Topaz
▨				#798	#131	#7022	Cornflower Blue Dk.
		●		#800	#144	#7020	Delft Pale
□				#973	#297	#2290	Canary Bright

Monarch
Stitch Count:
116 wide x 27 high

Approximate
Design Size:
11-count 10⅝" x 2½"
14-count 8⅜" x 2"
16-count 7¼" x 1¾"
18-count 6½" x 1½"
22-count 5⅜" x 1¼"

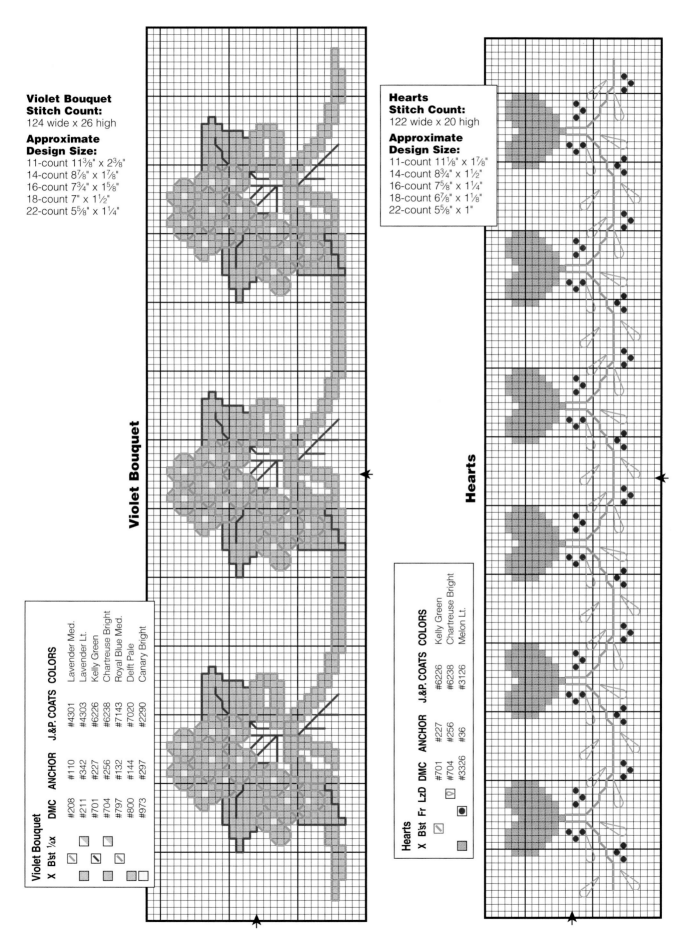

Violet Bouquet
Stitch Count:
124 wide x 26 high

Approximate Design Size:
11-count 11³⁄₈" x 2³⁄₈"
14-count 8⁷⁄₈" x 1⁷⁄₈"
16-count 7³⁄₄" x 1⁵⁄₈"
18-count 7" x 1½"
22-count 5⁵⁄₈" x 1¼"

Hearts
Stitch Count:
122 wide x 20 high

Approximate Design Size:
11-count 11⅛" x 1⁷⁄₈"
14-count 8³⁄₄" x 1½"
16-count 7⁵⁄₈" x 1¼"
18-count 6⁷⁄₈" x 1⅛"
22-count 5⁵⁄₈" x 1"

Violet Bouquet

X	Bst	¼x	DMC	ANCHOR	J.&P. COATS	COLORS
			#208	#110	#4301	Lavender Med.
			#211	#342	#4303	Lavender Lt.
			#701	#227	#6226	Kelly Green
			#704	#256	#6238	Chartreuse Bright
			#797	#132	#7143	Royal Blue Med.
			#800	#144	#7020	Delft Pale
			#973	#297	#2290	Canary Bright

Hearts

X	Bst	Fr	LzD	DMC	ANCHOR	J.&P. COATS	COLORS
				#701	#227	#6226	Kelly Green
				#704	#256	#6238	Chartreuse Bright
				#3326	#36	#3126	Melon Lt.

Floral Fingertip Towels

DESIGNED BY KATHLEEN HURLEY

MATERIALS:

Three ecru fingertip towels with a 2½" wide 14-count border

INSTRUCTIONS:

1: Center and stitch one design onto each towel, using two strands floss for Cross Stitch and one strand floss for Backstitch, Straight Stitch and French Knots. ❖

Pansies
Stitch Count:
118 wide x 28 high

Approximate Design Size:
11-count 10¾" x 2⅝"
14-count 8½" x 2"
16-count 7⅜" x 1¾"
18-count 6⅝" x 1⅝"
22-count 5⅝" x 1⅜"

Pansies

X	B'st	DMC	ANCHOR	JPC	COLORS
■	⁄	#310	#403	#8403	Black
■		#552	#112	#4092	Violet Med.
▨		#554	#96	#4104	Lavender Dk.
▨		#699	#923	#6228	Christmas Green
⧫		#702	#239	#6239	Parrot Green Dk.
▨		#704	#238	#6238	Chartreuse Bright
V		#712	#926	#5387	Cream
▨		#725	#305	#2298	Canary Deep
□		#727	#293	#2289	Topaz Very Lt.
▨		#781	#309	#5365	Brown Very Lt.
+		#783	#307	#5351	Tan
☒		#3031	#905	#5472	Coffee Brown Med.

Morning Glories

X	B'st	Fr	Str	DMC	ANCHOR	JPC	COLORS
		●	✓	#310	#403	#8403	Black
				#699	#923	#6228	Christmas Green
	✓			#704	#238	#6238	Chartreuse Bright
				#727	#293	#2289	Topaz Very Lt.
≈				#813	#160	#7161	Blue Lt.
				#825	#162	#7181	Blue Dk.
				#828	#158	#7053	Larkspur Lt.

Roses
Stitch Count:
122 wide x 25 high

Approximate Design Size:
11-count 11⅛" x 2⅜"
14-count 8¾" x 1⅞"
16-count 7⅝" x 1⅝"
18-count 6⅞" x 1⅜"
22-count 5⅝" x 1⅛"

Roses

X	B'st	DMC	ANCHOR	JPC	COLORS
◣	✓	#326	#39	#3401	Rose Ultra Deep
		#335	#38	#3283	Rose
		#367	#217	#6018	Pistachio Green Dk.
		#368	#214	#6016	Pistachio Green Lt.
+		#818	#23	#3281	Pink Med.
		#3326	#36	#3126	Melon Lt.

Morning Glories
Stitch Count:
124 wide x 28 high

Approximate Design Size:
11-count 11⅜" x 2⅝"
14-count 8⅞" x 2"
16-count 7¾" x 1¾"
18-count 7" x 1⅝"
22-count 5⅝" x 1⅜"

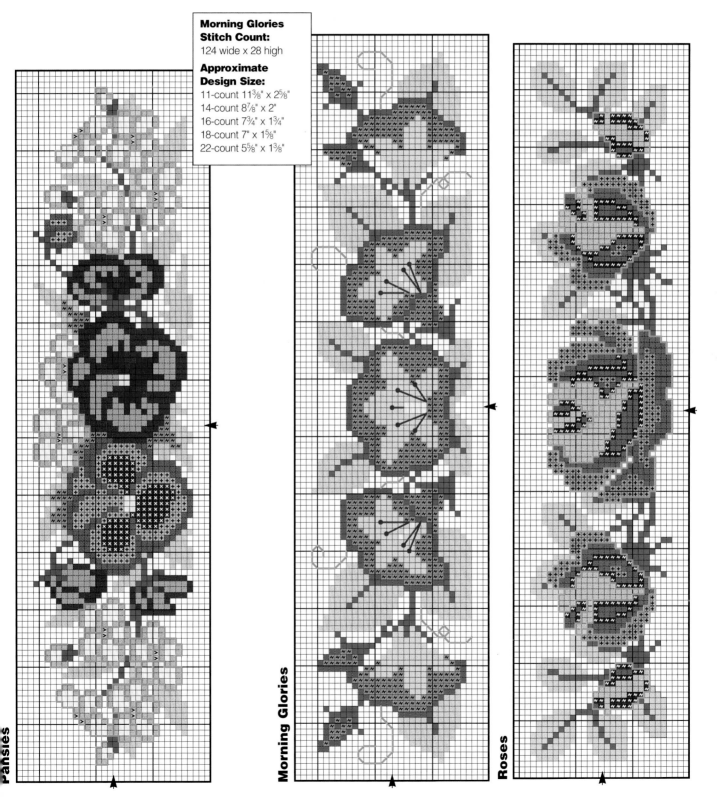

Pansies

Morning Glories

Roses

Powder Room Bouquet

Designed by Judy Chrispens

MATERIALS:

4" x 20" piece of ivory 18-count Aida; 4" x 5" ivory 14-count oval applique; 2¾" x 3½" ivory 18-count oval applique; Ivory terry hand towel and washcloth; Oval chipwood box; Craft glue or glue gun

INSTRUCTIONS:

NOTE: Measure width of hand towel to determine proper length needed.

1: Center and stitch Towel design onto 4" x 20" piece of Aida, and Washcloth design onto 2¾" x 3½" oval applique, using one strand floss for Cross Stitch and Backstitch. Center and stitch Bath Pearls design onto 4" x 5" oval applique, using two strands floss for Cross Stitch and one strand floss for Backstitch.

2: For towel, trim Towel design to fit width of purchased terry hand towel. Press under outside edges of stitched Aida; position and stitch onto towel.

3: For washcloth, position and stitch Washcloth applique onto terry washcloth as shown in photo.

4: For bath pearls box, decorate chipwood box as desired. Glue Bath Pearls applique on top of lid as shown in photo.

Towel

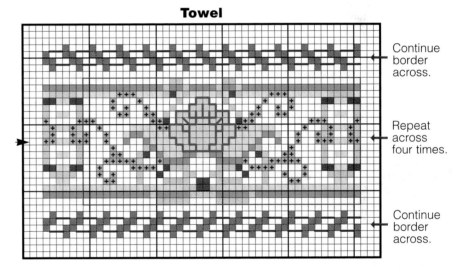

Continue border across.

Repeat across four times.

Continue border across.

Towel (one motif)
Stitch Count:
42 wide x 29 high

Approximate Design Size:
11-count 3⅞" x 2⅝"
14-count 3" x 2⅛"
16-count 2⅝" x 1⅞"
18-count 2⅜" x 1⅝"
22-count 2" x 1⅜"

Bath Pearls
Stitch Count:
40 wide x 19 high

Approximate Design Size:
11-count 3⅝" x 1¾"
14-count 2⅞" x 1⅜"
16-count 2½" x 1¼"
18-count 2¼" x 1⅛"
22-count 1⅞" x ⅞"

Washcloth
Stitch Count:
24 wide x 10 high

Approximate Design Size:
11-count 2¼" x 1"
14-count 1¾" x ¾"
16-count 1½" x ⅝"
18-count 1⅜" x ⅝"
22-count 1⅛" x ½"

Washcloth

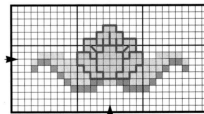

Bath Pearls

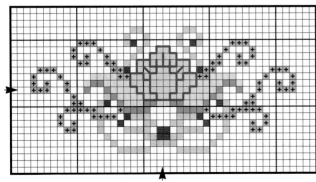

X	B'st	DMC	ANCHOR	JPC	COLORS
■		#351	#10	#3011	Coral
	✎	#353	#8	#3006	Peach Flesh Lt.
	✎	#420	#375	#5374	Brown Med.
+		#422	#373	#5372	Tan Very Lt.
		#472	#264	#6253	Avocado Green Ultra Lt.
		#746	#275	#1002	Off White
■		#3347	#266	#6266	Apple Green

Granny's Kitchen

Pour yourself a cup of tea,
find a sunny corner, and
remember the visions and
aromas of days gone by –
days when Grandma's oven
was full of homemade cookies
and her windowsills were
overflowing with fragrant,
fresh flowers …
each stitch in time, a warm
and tender memory of sunny
childhood days.

Sweetheart Kitchen

Instructions on next page

Sweetheart Kitchen

DESIGNED BY JUDY CHRISPENS

MATERIALS:

One 12" x 12" piece and one 8" x length needed for basket width of white 14-count Aida; ¼ yd. white vinyl weave; White hang towel; Basket; Canister set; Lucite™ recipe clip; ½ yd. cotton fabric; ⅛ yd. white batiste; 3¾ yds. blue ⅝" satin ribbon; 2 yds. white 1" flat eyelet; Double the length needed for basket width of white 1" flat eyelet; 1¾ yds. piping; Quilt batting; Craft glue or glue gun

CANISTER & BREAD TAGS
INSTRUCTIONS:

NOTES: From vinyl weave, cut five 6" x 6" pieces. Cut ribbon into four lengths to fit around canisters, one length to fit basket and eight 3" lengths for canister tag trim.

1: Center and stitch Tag design onto one vinyl weave piece, choosing desired label and using two strands floss for Cross Stitch and Backstitch. Repeat for remaining labels.

2: Trim each stitched vinyl weave piece following graph. Cut ribbon insertion. Insert one ribbon through cut areas as shown in photo. Tie around canister as shown. Glue two 3" ribbons to bottom of each canister tag; trim ends as desired.

HANG TOWEL
INSTRUCTIONS:

1: Center and stitch Hang Towel design onto hang towel, using two strands floss for Cross Stitch.

RECIPE CLIP
INSTRUCTIONS:

NOTES: From vinyl weave, cut one 6" x 7" piece. From ribbon, cut two 3" lengths.

1: Center and stitch Recipe Clip design, using two strands floss for Cross Stitch. Trim stitched vinyl weave following graph. Glue ribbons to bottom of vinyl weave; trim ends as desired. Glue onto front of Lucite™ recipe clip as desired.

POT HOLDER
INSTRUCTIONS:

NOTES: Trim stitched Aida to 7½" wide x 8" tall for front. From fabric, cut one 7½" x 8" piece for back, two 3½" x 36" pieces for ruffle and one 2" x 4" piece for hanging loop. From eyelet, cut one 72" length. From quilt batting, cut two 7½" x 8" pieces.

1: Center and stitch Pot Holder design onto 12" x 12" piece of Aida, using two strands floss for Cross Stitch.

2: For fabric ruffle, stitch short ends together, forming ring. Fold in half lengthwise; press. Stitch eyelet ends together, forming ring. Place on top of fabric ruffle. Gather unfinished edges to fit around outside edge of front. With right sides together and with ¼" seams, stitch to front, piping and ruffle.

3: Baste quilt batting to wrong side of front. With right sides together, stitch back to front, being careful not to stitch outside edge of ruffle in seam and leaving an opening. Turn right side out; press. Slip stitch opening closed.

4: With right sides together and with ¼" seams, fold hanging loop fabric in half lengthwise; stitch long edges together. Turn right side out; press. Fold in half and stitch at top center as shown in photo. Machine quilt around design.

BASKET TRIM
INSTRUCTIONS:

1: Stitch Basket Trim design onto 8" x desired length of Aida, repeating motifs across, using two strands floss for Cross Stitch.

NOTES: Trim stitched Aida to 3" tall by desired length to fit basket. From fabric, cut one 3" x double the length of bottom edge of stitched Aida for fabric ruffle. From batiste fabric, cut one piece same as stitched Aida for lining.

2: For fabric ruffle, with right sides together and with ¼" seams, stitch ends. Turn right sides out; press. Finish ends of eyelet. Place on top of fabric ruffle. Gather unfinished edges to fit bottom edge of stitched Aida. With right sides together, stitch to bottom edge, piping and ruffle.

3: With right sides together, stitch lining to stitched Aida, being careful not to stitch outside edge of ruffle in seam and leaving an opening. Turn right side out; press. Slip stitch opening closed. Glue basket trim to basket as shown in photo. ❖

Recipe Clip

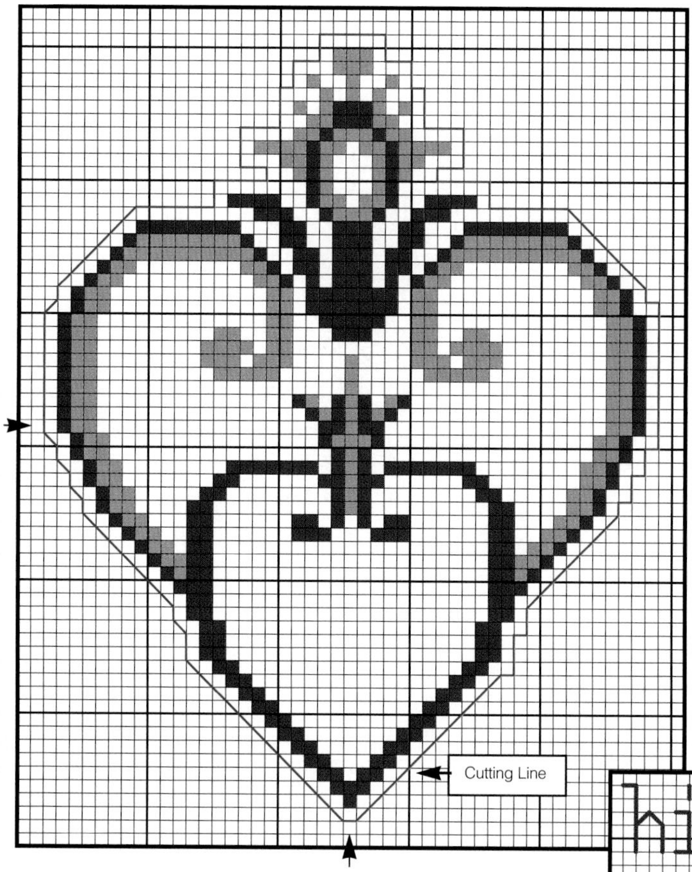

Recipe Clip
Stitch Count:
45 wide x 57 high

Approximate
Design Size:
11-count 4⅛" x 5¼"
14-count 3¼" x 4⅛"
16-count 2⅞" x 3⅝"
18-count 2½" x 3¼"
22-count 2⅛" x 2⅝"

Cutting Line →

X	B'st	DMC	ANCHOR	JPC	COLORS
■	✎	#798	#131	#7022	Cornflower Blue Dk.
▨		#799	#136	#7030	Blue

Tag Labels & Alphabet

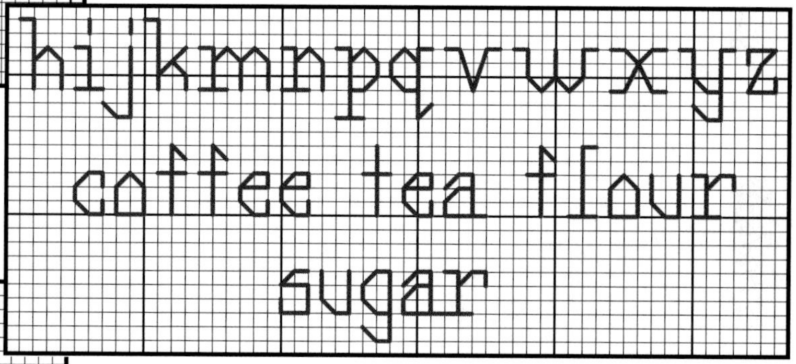

Tag

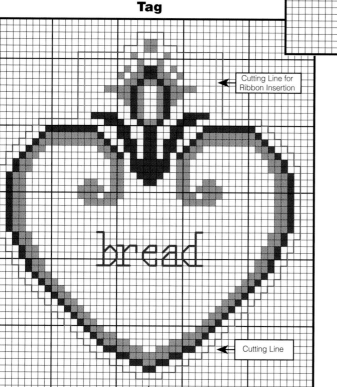

Cutting Line for
Ribbon Insertion →

Cutting Line →

Tag
Stitch Count:
44 wide x 50 high

Approximate
Design Size:
11-count 4" x 4⅝"
14-count 3¼" x 3⅝"
16-count 2¾" x 3⅛"
18-count 2½" x 2⅞"
22-count 2" x 2⅜"

Graphs continued on next page

Hang Towel

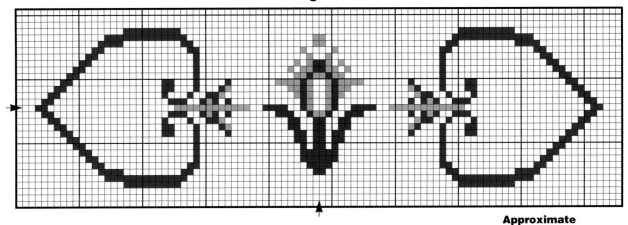

X	B'st	DMC	ANCHOR	JPC	COLORS
■	✓	#798	#131	#7022	Cornflower Blue Dk.
▨		#799	#136	#7030	Blue

Hang Towel Stitch Count:
90 wide x 25 high

Approximate Design Size:
11-count 8¼" x 2⅜"
14-count 6½" x 1⅞"
16-count 5⅝" x 1⅝"
18-count 5" x 1⅜"
22-count 4⅛" x 1⅛"

Basket Trim Stitch Count:
22 high

Approximate Design Size:
11-count 2"
14-count 1⅝"
16-count 1⅜"
18-count 1¼"
22-count 1"

Basket Trim

Pot Holder

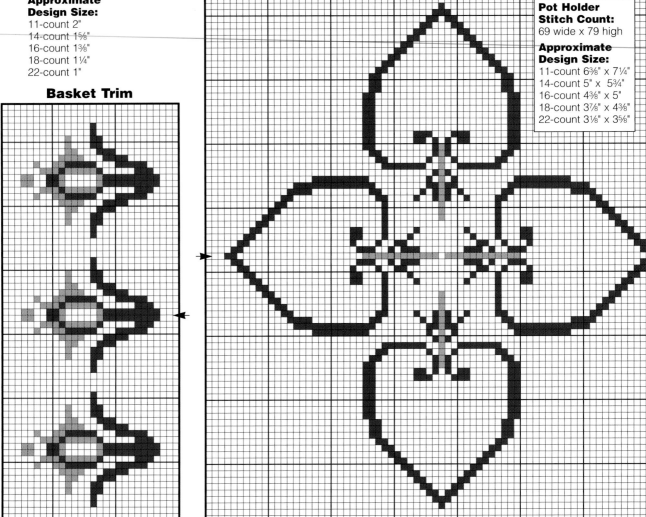

Pot Holder Stitch Count:
69 wide x 79 high

Approximate Design Size:
11-count 6⅜" x 7¼"
14-count 5" x 5¾"
16-count 4⅜" x 5"
18-count 3⅞" x 4⅜"
22-count 3⅛" x 3⅝"

Roses for Mother

Instructions on next page

Roses for Mother

DESIGNED BY JUDY CHRISPENS

MATERIALS:

One 16" x 16" piece, one 11" x 16" piece and one 9" x 11" piece of ice blue 28-count Annabelle; ½ yd. of 45" fabric; ⅞ yd. of ¼" satin ribbon; 5" x 7" white card with 3½" x 5" oval opening; ⅜ yd. each of piping and flat lace

INSTRUCTIONS:

1: For Tea Cozy, center and stitch Tea Cozy design onto 11" x 16" piece of Annabelle, stitching over two threads and using two strands floss for Cross Stitch and one strand floss for Backstitch.

NOTES: Centering design, trim stitched Tea Cozy design following Tea Cozy Pattern for front. From fabric, cut one piece following Tea Cozy Pattern for back; one 2" x 30" piece for ruffle; one 1" x 14½" strip for top of ruffle; and one 2"-wide bias strip measuring around curved edge of Tea Cozy. From ribbon, cut one 14½" piece for top of ruffle, one 13" piece for bow and one 4" piece for hanging loop.

2: Finish bottom edge of front and back pieces. For ruffle, fold in half lengthwise with wrong sides together; press. Gather ruffle to fit bottom edge of Tea Cozy front.

Press under ¼" along both long edges of strip for top of ruffle. Place ruffle and ruffle top to front matching bottom edges; stitch. Stitch 14½" ribbon on top of ruffle strip as shown in photo. Press under ¼" along both long edges of bias strip. Fold in half lengthwise with wrong sides together; press. With wrong sides together, baste front and back together along curved edges. Place bias trim over curved edge; stitch in place. Fold 4" piece of ribbon in half for hanging loop. Tie remaining ribbon into a bow. Tack hanging loop and ribbon to top of Tea Cozy as shown.

3: For Napkin, center and stitch Napkin design (omit "For Mother" in lower right corner) 1½" from edges, stitching over two threads and using two strands floss for Cross Stitch and one strand floss for Backstitch. To fray edges, stay stitch ⅝" from edges and separate crosswise threads with blunt end of needle.

4: For Gift Card, center and stitch Gift Card design onto 9" x 11" piece of Annabelle, stitching over two threads and using two strands floss for Backstitch. Glue piping, lace and stitched Annabelle to card as shown in photo.❖

Place on Fold

Tea Cozy Pattern
Front & Back

Tea Cozy

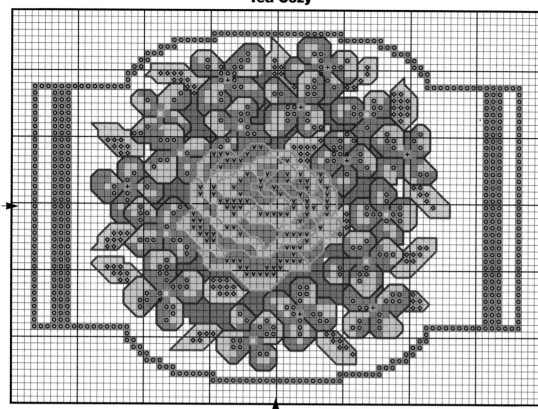

Tea Cozy Stitch Count:
74 wide x 53 high

Approximate Design Size:
11-count 6¾" x 4⅞"
14-count 5⅜" x 3⅞"
16-count 4⅝" x 3⅜"
18-count 4⅛" x 3"
22-count 3⅜" x 2½"
28-count over two
    threads 5⅜" x 3⅞"

Gift Card & Napkin

Gift Card Stitch Count:
41 wide x 58 high

Approximate Design Size:
11-count 3¾" x 5⅜"
14-count 3" x 4¼"
16-count 2⅝" x 3⅝"
18-count 2⅜" x 3¼"
22-count 1⅞" x 2⅝"
28-count over two
    threads 3"x 4¼"

Napkin Stitch Count:
41 wide x 42 high

Approximate Design Size:
11-count 3¾" x 3⅞"
14-count 3" x 3"
16-count 2⅝" x 2⅝"
18-count 2⅜" x 2⅜"
22-count 1⅞" x 2"
28-count over two
    threads 3" x 3"

X	B'st	¼x	DMC	ANCHOR	J.&P. COATS	COLORS
	✓		#315	#972	#3082	Antique Mauve Dk.
▨		▨	#340	#118	#7110	Blue Violet Med.
▢		▢	#341	#117	#7005	Blue Violet Lt.
+			#725	#311	#2298	Canary Deep
	✓		#780	#365	#5000	Russet
⊙		▨	#793	#176	#7978	Navy Blue Very Lt.
	✓		#797	#940	#7023	Blue Med.
◈		▨	#906	#257	#6256	Parrot Green Med.
	✓		#936	#269	#6269	Pine Green Dk.
▨		▨	#937	#268	#6268	Avocado Green Med. Dk.
▢			#3078	#292	#2292	Golden Yellow Very Lt.
▢		▨	#3347	#266	#6266	Apple Green
▢		▨	#3713	#968	#3068	Salmon Lt.
▨		▨	#3726	#970	#3082	Antique Mauve Dk.
ⱽ		▨	#3727	#969	#3081	Antique Mauve Med.

Instructions on page 84

Luscious
Fruit

Luscious Fruit

DESIGNED BY NANCY MARSHALL

MATERIALS:

1⅛ yds. of denim blue 22-count Kitchen Hardanger; Container with round lid (3⅜" x 3⅜" design area); Thin cardboard; Craft glue or glue gun

NOTE: From Hardanger, for towel and bread cloth, cut two squares around three bold parallel lines leaving 1½" excess for hemming or fraying; for lid, cut one 9" x 9" piece.

INSTRUCTIONS:
TOWEL

1: Position and stitch Towel design onto one square of Hardanger, leaving one row of squares on end and two rows of squares on each side unstitched. Stitch over two threads, using three strands floss for Cross Stitch and Backstitch. Narrowly hem unfinished edges.

BREAD CLOTH

1: Position and stitch Bread Cloth design diagonally onto each corner of one square of Hardanger following graph. Stitch over two threads, using three strands floss for Cross Stitch and Backstitch. Trim edges ¾" from bold parallel lines; fray edges.

LID

1: Center and stitch lid design onto 9" x 9" piece of Hardanger, stitching over two threads and using three strands floss for Cross Stitch and Backstitch.

2: Cut cardboard to fit inside lid. Center stitched Hardanger on top of cardboard. Trim Hardanger edge to 1" larger than cardboard; fold edge back and glue to secure. Position and secure in lid.❖

Bread Cloth & Lid
Stitch Count:
24 wide x 26 high
Approximate Design Size:
11-count 2¼" x 2⅜"
14-count 1¾" x 1⅞"
16-count 1½" x 1⅝"
18-count 1⅜" x 1½"
22-count 1⅛" x 1¼"
22-count over two
   threads 2¼" x 2⅜"

Towel
Stitch Count:
78 wide x 29 high
Approximate Design Size:
11-count 7⅛" x 2⅝"
14-count 5⅝" x 2⅛"
16-count 4⅞" x 1⅞"
18-count 4⅜" x 1⅝"
22-count 3⅝" x 1⅜"
22-count over
   two threads 7⅛" x 2⅝"

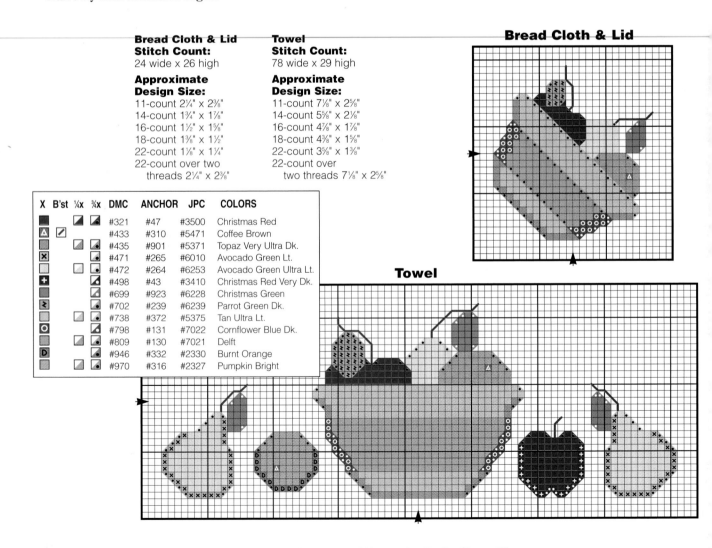

X	B'st	¼x	¾x	DMC	ANCHOR	JPC	COLORS
				#321	#47	#3500	Christmas Red
				#433	#310	#5471	Coffee Brown
				#435	#901	#5371	Topaz Very Ultra Dk.
				#471	#265	#6010	Avocado Green Lt.
				#472	#264	#6253	Avocado Green Ultra Lt.
				#498	#43	#3410	Christmas Red Very Dk.
				#699	#923	#6228	Christmas Green
				#702	#239	#6239	Parrot Green Dk.
				#738	#372	#5375	Tan Ultra Lt.
				#798	#131	#7022	Cornflower Blue Dk.
				#809	#130	#7021	Delft
				#946	#332	#2330	Burnt Orange
				#970	#316	#2327	Pumpkin Bright

Bread Cloth & Lid

Towel

Hearts & Tulips

Instructions on next page

Hearts & Tulips

DESIGNED BY VIRGINIA G. SOSKIN

MATERIALS FOR SET:

One pink terry towel, pot holder and oven mitt; 10" x 10" piece of antique white 14-count Aida; ½ yd. white 1" pre-gathered eyelet; Container with heart lid; Polyester batting; Thin cardboard; Craft glue or glue gun

INSTRUCTIONS:

1: Center and stitch corresponding designs on towel, potholder, oven mitt and Aida, using two strands floss for Cross Stitch. Use one strand floss for Backstitch of dove and French Knots. Use two strands floss for remaining Backstitch.

2: For lid, cut cardboard to fit inside lid. Place polyester batting on top of cardboard; trim to fit. Center wrong side of stitched Aida on top of batting and cardboard. Trim Aida edges to 1" larger than cardboard; fold edges back and glue to secure. Mount in lid. Glue eyelet under lid edge.❖

Jar Lid Cover

Jar Lid Stitch Count:
46 wide x 42 high

Approximate Design Size:
11-count 4¼" x 3⅞"
14-count 3⅜" x 3"
16-count 2⅞" x 2⅝"
18-count 2⅝" x 2⅜"
22-count 2⅛" x 2"

Towel Stitch Count:
180 wide x 35 high

Approximate Design Size:
11-count 16⅜" x 3¼"
14-count 12⅞" x 2½"
16-count 11¼ x 2¼"
18-count 10" x 2"
22-count 8¼" x 1⅝"

Towel

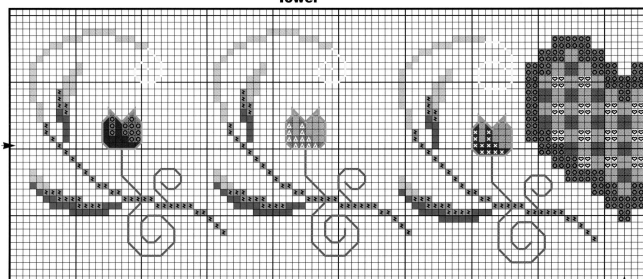

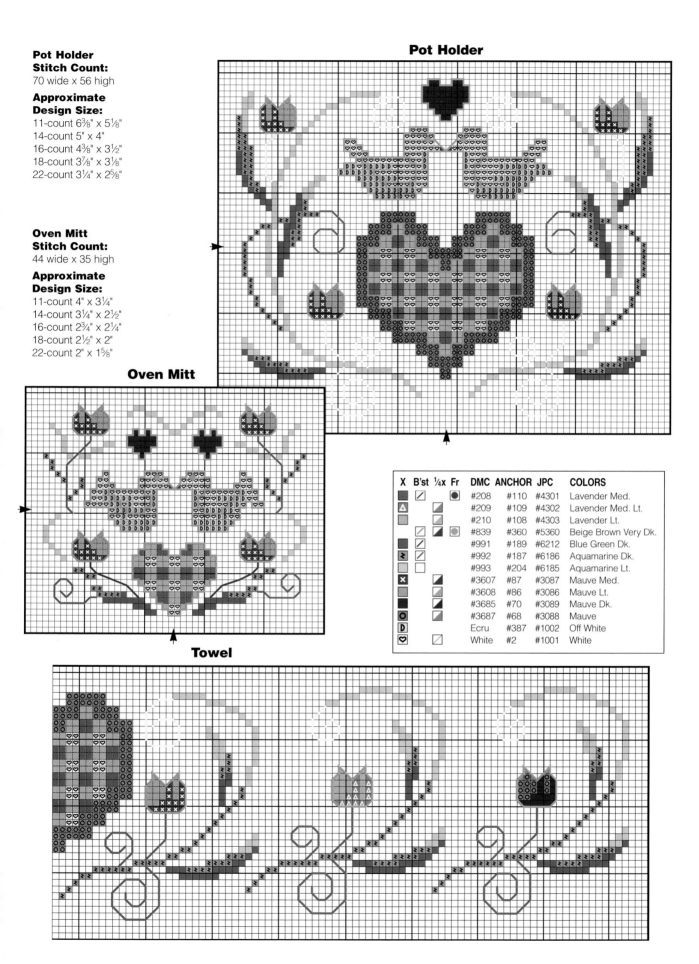

Pot Holder

Pot Holder Stitch Count:
70 wide x 56 high

Approximate Design Size:
11-count 6⅜" x 5⅛"
14-count 5" x 4"
16-count 4⅜" x 3½"
18-count 3⅞" x 3⅛"
22-count 3¼" x 2⅝"

Oven Mitt Stitch Count:
44 wide x 35 high

Approximate Design Size:
11-count 4" x 3¼"
14-count 3¼" x 2½"
16-count 2¾" x 2¼"
18-count 2½" x 2"
22-count 2" x 1⅝"

Oven Mitt

Towel

X	B'st	¼x	Fr	DMC	ANCHOR	JPC	COLORS
			●	#208	#110	#4301	Lavender Med.
△				#209	#109	#4302	Lavender Med. Lt.
				#210	#108	#4303	Lavender Lt.
			●	#839	#360	#5360	Beige Brown Very Dk.
				#991	#189	#6212	Blue Green Dk.
≥				#992	#187	#6186	Aquamarine Dk.
				#993	#204	#6185	Aquamarine Lt.
✕				#3607	#87	#3087	Mauve Med.
				#3608	#86	#3086	Mauve Lt.
				#3685	#70	#3089	Mauve Dk.
O				#3687	#68	#3088	Mauve
D				Ecru	#387	#1002	Off White
♡				White	#2	#1001	White

Family Dinner

Instructions on page 90

Family Dinner

DESIGNED BY HOLLIE DESIGNS, JUDY M. GIBBS

MATERIALS:

Table runner; Bread basket cover; 5" x 8" off-white pre-made pillow hanging; Fiberfill

INSTRUCTIONS:

1: Center and stitch designs on table runner and bread basket cover, using two strands floss for Cross Stitch and one strand floss for Backstitch.

2: Center and stitch design on pillow hanging, working each stitch over two threads on linen, using two strands floss for Cross Stitch and one strand floss for Backstitch. Slip stitch opening closed. ❖

Pillow Hanging
Stitch Count:
58 wide x 98 high

Approximate Design Size:
11-count 5⅜" x 9"
14-count 4¼" x 7"
16-count 3⅝" x 6⅛"
18-count 3¼" x 5½"
22-count 2⅝" x 4½"

Pillow Hanging

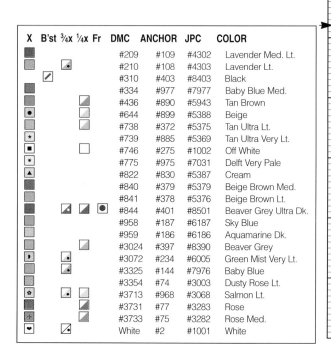

X	B'st	¾x	¼x	Fr	DMC	ANCHOR	JPC	COLOR
					#209	#109	#4302	Lavender Med. Lt.
					#210	#108	#4303	Lavender Lt.
					#310	#403	#8403	Black
					#334	#977	#7977	Baby Blue Med.
					#436	#890	#5943	Tan Brown
					#644	#899	#5388	Beige
					#738	#372	#5375	Tan Ultra Lt.
					#739	#885	#5369	Tan Ultra Very Lt.
					#746	#275	#1002	Off White
					#775	#975	#7031	Delft Very Pale
					#822	#830	#5387	Cream
					#840	#379	#5379	Beige Brown Med.
					#841	#378	#5376	Beige Brown Lt.
					#844	#401	#8501	Beaver Grey Ultra Dk.
					#958	#187	#6187	Sky Blue
					#959	#186	#6186	Aquamarine Dk.
					#3024	#397	#8390	Beaver Grey
					#3072	#234	#6005	Green Mist Very Lt.
					#3325	#144	#7976	Baby Blue
					#3354	#74	#3003	Dusty Rose Lt.
					#3713	#968	#3068	Salmon Lt.
					#3731	#77	#3283	Rose
					#3733	#75	#3282	Rose Med.
					White	#2	#1001	White

Table Runner

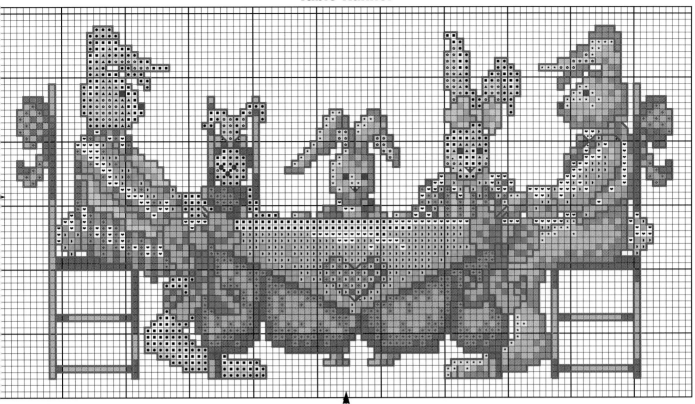

Table Runner
Stitch Count:
103 wide x 55 high

Approximate Design Size:
11-count 9⅜" x 5"
14-count 7⅜" x 4"
16-count 6½" x 3½"
18-count 5¾" x 3⅛"
22-count 4¾" x 2½"

Bread Basket Cover
Stitch Count:
64 wide x 71 high
Approximate Design Size:
11-count 5⅞" x 6½"
14-count 4⅝" x 5⅛"
16-count 4" x 4½"
18-count 3⅝" x 4"
22-count 3" x 3¼"

Enjoy cuddly critters stitched on thirsty terrycloth towels – they appear again to adorn a heartwarming sampler.

Love Warms the Heart

DESIGNED BY FELICIA L. WILLIAMS

MATERIALS:

12" x 14" piece of platinum 14-count Aida; Three rose check terry towels with a 3¼" 14-count border

INSTRUCTIONS:

NOTE: For towels, choose motifs of choice from graph and chart on graph paper for proper placement.

1: For Sampler, center and stitch design onto 12" x 14" piece of Aida, using three strands floss for Cross Stitch and one strand floss for Backstitch and French Knots.

2: For Towels, center and stitch motifs of choice onto each towel, using three strands floss for Cross Stitch and one strand floss for Backstitch and French Knots.❖

Stitch Count:
82 wide x 106 high

Approximate Design Size:
11-count 7½" x 9⅝"
14-count 5⅞" x 7⅝"
16-count 5⅛" x 6⅝"
18-count 4⅝" x 6"
22-count 3¾" x 4⅞"

X	DMC	ANCHOR	J.&P. COATS	COLORS	X	B'st	Fr	DMC	ANCHOR	J.&P. COATS	COLORS
■	#315	#972	#3082	Antique Mauve Dk.	S			#758	#868	#2337	Terra Cotta Lt.
O	#316	#969	#3081	Antique Mauve Med.	V			#778	#969	#3080	Antique Mauve Lt.
	#562	#210	#6213	Jade Medium	≋			#822	#830	#5387	Cream
X	#632	#936	#5470	Brown				#840	#379	#5379	Beige Brown Med.
+	#642	#832	#5393	Beige Grey Very Dk.	■			#844	#273	#8501	Beaver Grey Ultra Dk.
	#644	#899	#5388	Beige				#926	#850	#6007	Green Mist Med.
D	#647	#8581	#8900	Beaver Grey Med.	□			#3042	#870	#4221	Antique Violet Lt.
	#754	#6	#2331	Peach Flesh Very Lt.	Λ	⁄	●	#3371	#382	#5478	Brown Very Ultra Dk.

Precious Years

Welcome that precious new
baby with a lovingly
handstitched gift. What better
way to remember a special
"birth" day than with
the favorite motifs of
childhood – bears and
bunnies and bows, hearts
and lambs ...
each stitch a legacy of
enduring love from the heart
of the stitcher, a heart as soft
as a newborn's smile.

Sugar & Spice

Instructions on next page

Sugar & Spice

DESIGNED BY JUDY CHRISPENS

MATERIALS:

One 12" x 12" piece of carnation and one 12" x 12" piece of periwinkle 28-count pastel linen; ½ yd. of fabric; 1 yd. of ⅜" satin ribbon; ¾" tall wooden letters; Polyester fiberfill; Craft glue or glue gun

INSTRUCTIONS:

1: Center and stitch Dolly design onto carnation linen and Teddy design onto periwinkle linen, stitching over two threads and using two strands floss for Cross Stitch and one strand floss for Backstitch.

NOTES: Open album and measure. From fabric, for cover, cut one piece same size plus ½" around for seam allowance. For lining, cut two pieces same size as front and back, plus ½" around for seam allowances. For outside ruffle, cut fabric strips 2"

Dolly

X	B'st	DMC	ANCHOR	JPC	COLORS
D		#208	#110	#4301	Lavender Med.
	✎	#300	#352	#5349	Golden Brown Dk.
	✎	#311	#148	#7980	Navy Blue Med.
+		#353	#8	#3006	Peach Flesh Lt.
		#581	#266	#6256	Parrot Green Med.
≷		#754	#6	#3239	Shell Pink Lt.
	✎	#758	#868	#2337	Terra Cotta Lt.
✕		#794	#175	#7977	Baby Blue Med.
		#800	#129	#7020	Delft Pale
	✎	#899	#55	#3282	Rose Med.
	✎	#917	#89	#3088	Mauve
		#920	#339	#2326	Copper
▲		#921	#338	#3337	Terra Cotta Lt.
		#922	#337	#3336	Terra Cotta Very Lt.
		#948	#778	#2331	Peach Flesh Very Lt.
		#3607	#87	#3088	Mauve
		#3608	#86	#3087	Mauve Med.

Dolly

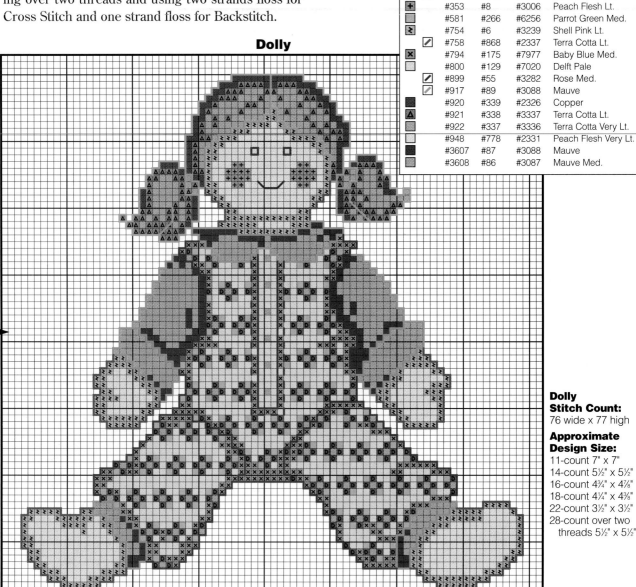

**Dolly
Stitch Count:**
76 wide x 77 high
**Approximate
Design Size:**
11-count 7" x 7"
14-count 5½" x 5½"
16-count 4¾" x 4⅞"
18-count 4¼" x 4⅜"
22-count 3½" x 3½"
28-count over two
    threads 5½" x 5½"

wide x double the outside edge of album measurement. For frame ruffle, cut fabric strips 1½" wide x double the inside frame cutout measurement. From cardboard, for frame, cut one piece same size as album front with 6⅛" x 6⅛" square cut out of center.

2: For inside lining of album, finish one long edge on each lining piece. Place finished edges of each lining piece close to spine on inside front and back of album cover. Fold seams around outside edges of album; glue to secure. Sew matching ruffle strips together, forming rings; finish one long edge on each. Gather 2"-wide ring to fit around outside edge of album cover. With right sides together and with ½" seams,

stitch in place.

3: Trim polyester batting to fit cardboard frame and album back, glue in place. Position frame onto front of album. Cut an opening 1" smaller than cutout of cardboard frame on front of fabric cover. Position on top of cardboard frame, clip corners and fold back 1"; glue to back of frame. Gather 1½"-wide ring to fit inside frame; glue ½" to inside edge of ruffle. Tack outside edge of ruffle to hold in place.

4: Center stitched design into frame opening, glue onto album front. Fold under ½" seam allowance; glue cover onto album as shown in photo. Glue wooden letters above and below frame and bows at corners as shown.❖

Teddy

X	B'st	DMC	ANCHOR	JPC	COLORS
✖	✎	#310	#403	#8403	Black
		#746	#275	#1002	Off White
		#780	#365	#5000	Russet
		#781	#309	#5371	Topaz Very Ultra Dk.
		#782	#308	#5365	Brown Very Lt.
		#826	#161	#7180	Blue Med.

Teddy

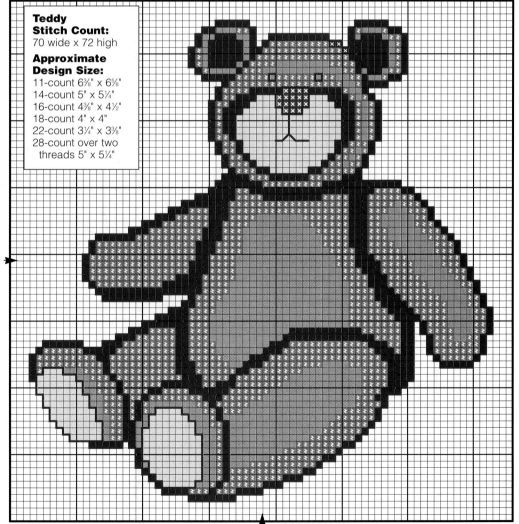

**Teddy
Stitch Count:**
70 wide x 72 high

**Approximate
Design Size:**
11-count 6⅜" x 6⅝"
14-count 5" x 5¼"
16-count 4⅜" x 4½"
18-count 4" x 4"
22-count 3¼" x 3⅜"
28-count over two
  threads 5" x 5¼"

Little fingers
little toes
Tiny mouth &
tiny nose
Disposition
gentle, mild
God bless you
Oh precious child.

Derek John

Precious Child

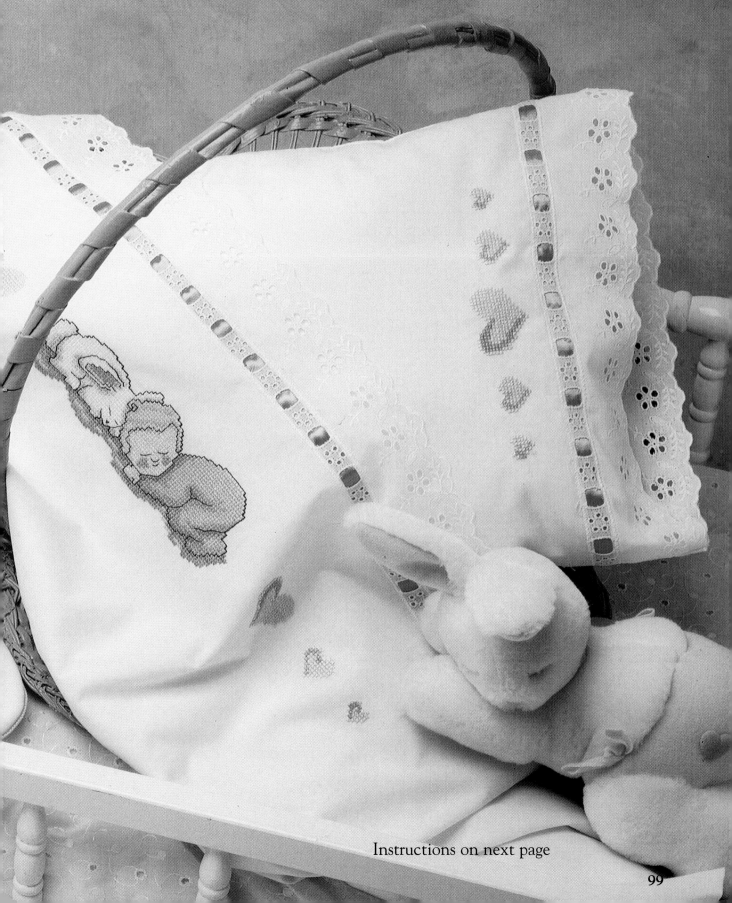

Instructions on next page

Precious Child

DESIGNED BY MONA ENO

MATERIALS:

17" x 18" piece of white 11-count Aida; Frame with 14⅝" x 16¾" opening; White flat crib sheet; White crib pillowcase; 14-count waste canvas; Foam core board; Craft glue or glue gun

INSTRUCTIONS:

NOTES: Double mat was cut at a local frame shop. Chart desired motifs from sampler graph onto graph paper for crib sheet and pillowcase borders.

1: For Sampler, choosing letters from Alphabet graph for name, center and stitch design onto 17" x 18" piece of Aida, using three strands floss for Cross Stitch. Use two strands floss for Backstitch of lettering and one strand floss for remaining Backstitch.

2: For Crib Sheet and Pillowcase, apply waste canvas to top of sheet and edge of pillowcase, following manufacturer's instructions. Center and stitch design, using two strands floss for Cross Stitch and one strand floss for Backstitch. Remove waste canvas from crib sheet and pillowcase after stitching following manufacturer's instructions. ❖

Alphabet

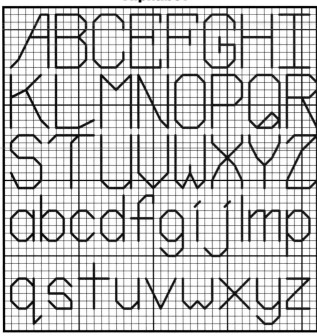

X	B'st	¼x	¾x	DMC	ANCHOR	J.&P. COATS	COLORS
	✎			#208	#110	#4301	Lavender Med.
				#209	#109	#4302	Lavender Med. Lt.
∧				#210	#108	#4104	Lavender Dk.
				#211	#342	#4303	Lavender Lt.
		◪		#415	#398	#8398	Silver
∨				#676	#891	#2305	Wheat Straw
				#677	#886	#5372	Tan Very Lt.
⊠				#754	#1012	#2331	Peach Flesh Very Lt.
▢		◪		#762	#234	#8510	Pearl Grey Very Lt.
∫				#818	#23	#3281	Pink Med.
		◪		#912	#209	#6226	Kelly Green
⇄				#913	#204	#6225	Nile
	✎			#938	#381	#5381	Mocha Brown Very Dk.
				#948	#1011	#2331	Peach Flesh Very Lt.
				#955	#206	#6020	Nile Green
⊙				#958	#187	#6186	One strand Aquamarine Dk. held together with
				#964	#185	#6185	Two strands Aquamarine Lt.
✚				#958	#187	#6186	Two strands Aquamarine Dk. held together with
				#964	#185	#6185	One strand Aquamarine Lt.
				#964	#185	#6185	Aquamarine Lt.
			◪	#3326	#36	#3126	Melon Lt.
♡		◪		White	#2	#1001	White

Little fingers
little toes
Tiny mouth &
tiny nose
Disposition
gentle, mild
God bless you
Oh precious child.

Derek John

Stitch Count:
115 wide x 133 high
Approximate
Design Size:
11-count 10½" x 12⅛"
14-count 8¼" x 9½"
16-count 7¼" x 8⅜"
18-count 6⅜" x 7⅜"
22-count 5¼" x 6⅛"

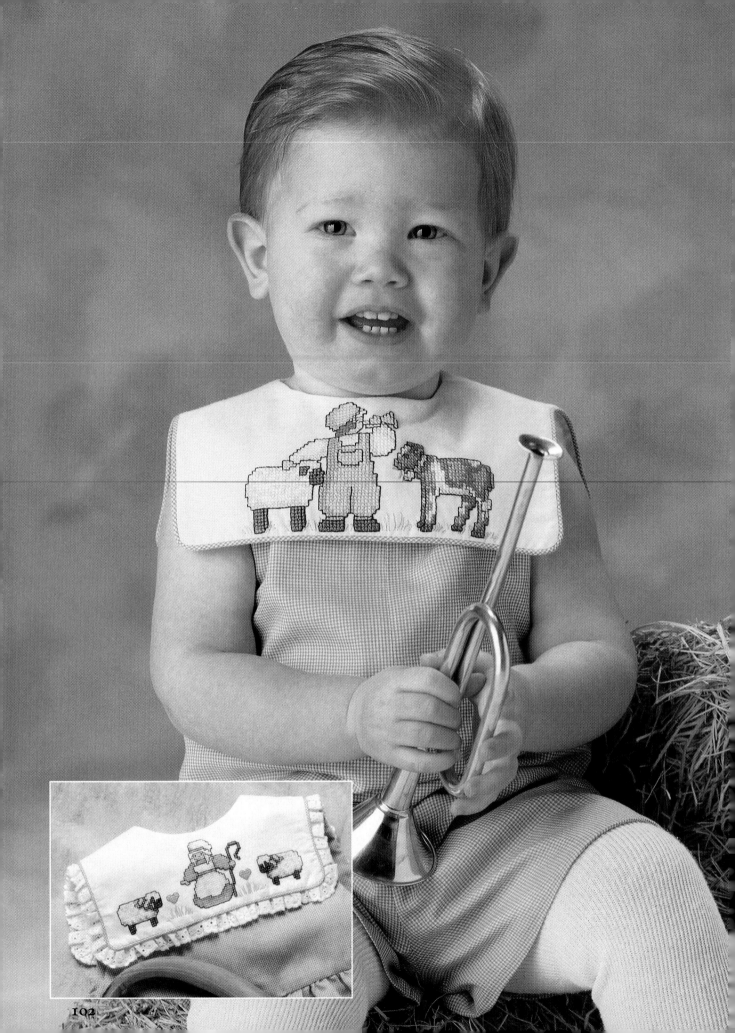

Nursery Rhymes

Designed by Jacquelyn Fox

COLLARS
MATERIALS FOR ONE:

5" x 7" piece of 14-count waste canvas; ¼ yd. white cotton fabric; 1⅛ yds. narrow piping; 3 yds. white ½" flat eyelet (for girl's collar); ¼" shank button; Washable fabric pen

INSTRUCTIONS:

1: Apply waste canvas onto fabric following manufacturer's instructions. Center and stitch Little Boy Blue design for boy's collar or Little Bo Peep design for girl's collar, using two strands floss for Cross Stitch and Backstitch. Remove waste canvas after stitching following manufacturer's instructions.

2: Using washable fabric pen, trace collar front onto fabric, being sure to center design. Cut one piece same as collar front for lining. Cut out four collar back pieces.

3: With right sides together and with ¼" seams, stitch front and back collar pieces together at shoulder seams. Repeat with lining pieces. With right sides, together, stitch piping around outside edge of collar, not including neck opening. For girl's collar, gather eyelet and stitch on top of piping.

4: With right sides together and ¼" seams, stitch collar front and lining together, leaving an opening. Turn right side out; press. Slip stitch opening closed. Sew button to left collar back. Make button loop on right collar back.❖

Graphs on next page

Collar Back
(cut 4)

SIZE 6
SIZE 4
SIZE 2
SIZE 6
SIZE 4
SIZE 2

Place on Fold
Place on Fold

Collar Front
(cut 2)

Little Boy Blue Stitch Count:
75 wide x 42 high

Approximate Design Size:
11-count 6⅞" x 3⅞"
14-count 5⅜" x 3"
16-count 4¾" x 2⅝"
18-count 4¼" x 2⅜"
22-count 3½" x 2"

Little Bo Peep Stitch Count:
95 wide x 33 high

Approximate Design Size:
11-count 8⅝" x 3"
14-count 6⅞" x 2⅜"
16-count 6" x 2⅛"
18-count 5⅜" x 1⅞"
22-count 4⅜" x 1½"

Little Bo Peep

X	¾x	Str	DMC	ANCHOR	J.&P. COATS	COLORS		X	B'st	¾x	Fr	DMC	ANCHOR	J.&P. COATS	COLORS
			#209	#109	#4302	Lavender Med. Lt.					#762	#397	#8510	Pearl Grey Very Lt.
			#210	#108	#4303	Lavender Lt.					#775	#975	#7031	Delft Very Pale
			#317	#400	#8512	Pewter Grey					#840	#379	#5379	Beige Brown Med.
			#318	#399	#8511	Steel Grey Lt.					#961	#76	#3153	Geranium
			#334	#977	#7977	Baby Blue Med.					#3325	#144	#7976	Baby Blue
			#563	#208	#6210	Jade Lt.					#3371	#382	#5478	Brown Very Ultra Dk.
			#745	#300	#2296	Yellow Pale					#3716	#25	#3150	Dusty Rose Very Lt.
			#754	#6	#2331	Peach Flesh Very Lt.					White	#2	#1001	White

Little Boy Blue

X	¾x	Str	DMC	ANCHOR	J.&P. COATS	COLORS		X	B'st	Fr	DMC	ANCHOR	J.&P. COATS	COLORS
			#317	#400	#8512	Pewter Grey					#762	#397	#8510	Pearl Grey Very Lt.
			#415	#398	#8511	Steel Grey Lt.					#3371	#382	#5478	Brown Very Ultra Dk.
			#563	#208	#6210	Jade Lt.					#3761	#9159	#7159	Blue Very Lt.
			#727	#293	#2289	Topaz Very Lt.					#3766	#167	#7167	Sky Blue
			#745	#300	#2296	Yellow Pale					#3772	#379	#5379	Beige Brown Med.
			#754	#6	#2331	Peach Flesh Very Lt.					#3773	#882	#5345	Spice Med.
			#760	#9	#3069	Salmon					White	#2	#1001	White

Let's Go Out

Instructions on next page

Let's Go Out

DESIGNED BY JUDY CHRISPENS

MATERIALS:

⅜ yd. of pistachio 28-count pastel linen; ½ yd. of 45" contrasting fabric; ⅜ yd. crisp iron-on backing material; 1½ yds. narrow cording; Fray preventer

INSTRUCTIONS:

NOTES: All seams are ½" unless otherwise noted. From pastel linen, cut two 9½" x 10½" pieces for front and back, two 4" x 9½" pieces for sides and one 4" x 10½" piece for bottom. Apply fray preventer to outside edges; allow to dry. From contrasting fabric, cut same as front, back, sides and bottom pieces for lining, and cut two 3" x 14" pieces for handles, one 2" x 24" bias strip for top trim and two 1½" x 27" bias strips for piping covering. From backing material, cut same as front, back, sides, bottom and handles.

1: Center and stitch design onto one 9½" x 10½" pastel linen piece, stitching over two threads and using two strands floss for Cross Stitch and one strand floss for Backstitch.

2: Iron backing material to wrong sides of front, back, sides, bottom and handles following manufacturer's instructions. For piping, cut cording into two 27" lengths. Fold each 1½" x 27" bias strip in half lengthwise wrong sides together with cording between. Using a zipper foot, stitch close to cording, forming piping. With right sides together, stitch piping to front and back along sides and bottom.

3: With right sides together, stitch front, back and sides together, stopping ½" from bottom. With right sides together, stitch bottom piece to bottom opening, turning fabric as you stitch each side. Turn right side out; press. Repeat with lining pieces, omitting backing material; do not turn right side out. With wrong sides together, place lining inside Tote; baste top edges together.

4: With right sides together, fold each handle piece in half lengthwise; stitch long edges together. Turn right sides out; press. With unfinished edges even, position one handle on front and one handle on back at top edges of Tote; baste in place.

5: For top trim, with right sides together, stitch short ends of 2" x 24" bias strip together, forming ring. Press under ½" along one long edge. Holding right sides together and unfinished edges even, stitch bias strip to top edge of Tote. Fold bias strip over top edge and slip stitch in place. ❖

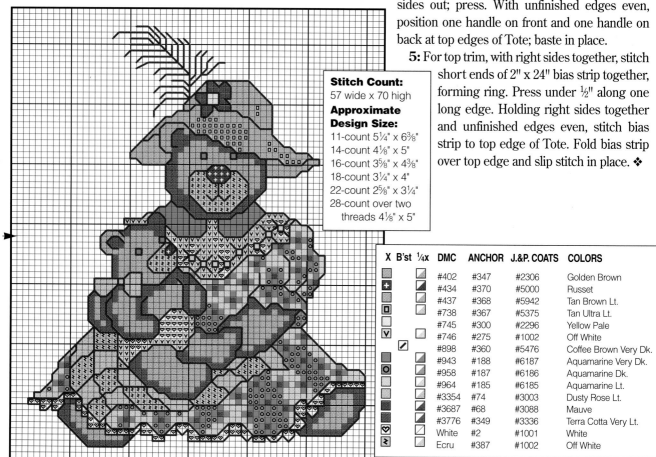

Stitch Count:
57 wide x 70 high

Approximate Design Size:
11-count 5¼" x 6⅜"
14-count 4⅛" x 5"
16-count 3⅝" x 4⅜"
18-count 3¼" x 4"
22-count 2⅝" x 3¼"
28-count over two
  threads 4⅛" x 5"

X	B'st	¼x	DMC	ANCHOR	J.&P. COATS	COLORS
			#402	#347	#2306	Golden Brown
+			#434	#370	#5000	Russet
			#437	#368	#5942	Tan Brown Lt.
▣			#738	#367	#5375	Tan Ultra Lt.
			#745	#300	#2296	Yellow Pale
V			#746	#275	#1002	Off White
			#898	#360	#5476	Coffee Brown Very Dk.
			#943	#188	#6187	Aquamarine Very Dk.
⊙			#958	#187	#6186	Aquamarine Dk.
			#964	#185	#6185	Aquamarine Lt.
			#3354	#74	#3003	Dusty Rose Lt.
			#3687	#68	#3088	Mauve
			#3776	#349	#3336	Terra Cotta Very Lt.
♥			White	#2	#1001	White
⊠			Ecru	#387	#1002	Off White

Lock of Baby's Hair

ANGELA MARIE

JULY 15, 1990

Instructions on next page

Lock of Baby's Hair

DESIGNED BY SHARON MOONEY

MATERIALS:

12" x 14" piece of white 14-count Aida; ⅛ yd. of ⅛" satin ribbon; Lock of baby's hair; Craft glue or glue gun

INSTRUCTIONS:

1: Choosing letters and numbers of choice, center and stitch design, using two strands floss for Cross Stitch. Tie ribbon into a bow; trim ends. Glue lock of hair onto sampler as indicated; glue bow over lock of hair as shown in photo.❖

Alphabet

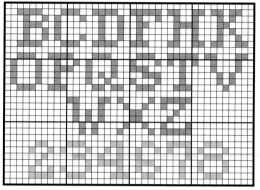

Stitch Count:
98 wide x 69 high

Approximate Design Size:
11-count 9" x 6⅜"
14-count 7" x 5"
16-count 6⅛" x 4⅜"
18-count 5½" x 3⅞"
22-count 4½" x 3⅛"

X	DMC	ANCHOR	JPC	COLORS
▨	#368	#214	#6016	Pistachio Green Lt.
■	#3350	#59	#3004	Dusty Rose Very Dk.
▨	#3354	#74	#3003	Dusty Rose Lt.
▨	#3747	#120	#7020	Delft Pale

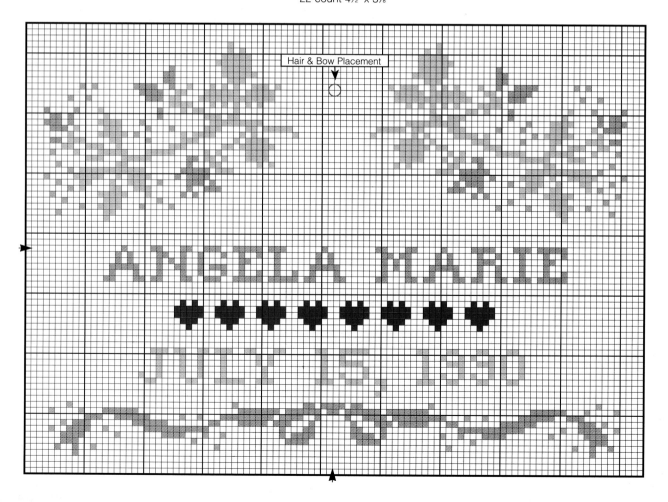

Hair & Bow Placement

Baby Plaids

Instructions on next page

Baby Plaids

DESIGNED BY JUDY CHRISPENS

MATERIALS:

12" x 13" piece of white 11-count Aida; 30" x 36" baby blanket with 6½" x 6½" 16-count corner squares; ⅝ yd. 45" fabric; ½ yd. coordinating 45" fabric; 1⅛ yds. cording; Polyester fiberfill

INSTRUCTIONS:

1: Center and stitch Heart design onto 12" x 13" piece of Aida and one Horse design in each corner of baby blanket, using two strands floss for Cross Stitch and one strand floss for Backstitch.

NOTES: Trim stitched Aida to 10⅝" wide x 9⅛" tall

for pillow front. From fabric, cut one 9⅛" x 10⅝" for pillow back and two 5" x 45" pieces for ruffle. From coordinating fabric, cut one 1½" x 41" bias strip for piping covering and one 2" x 90" bias strip for outside ruffle trim, piecing as needed.

2: For piping, fold 1½" x 41" bias strip in half lengthwise wrong sides together with cording between. Using a zipper foot, stitch close to cording. With right sides together and with ½" seam, stitch piping around pillow front.

3: With right sides together and with ½" seams, stitch short edges of 5" x 45" pieces together, forming

Heart

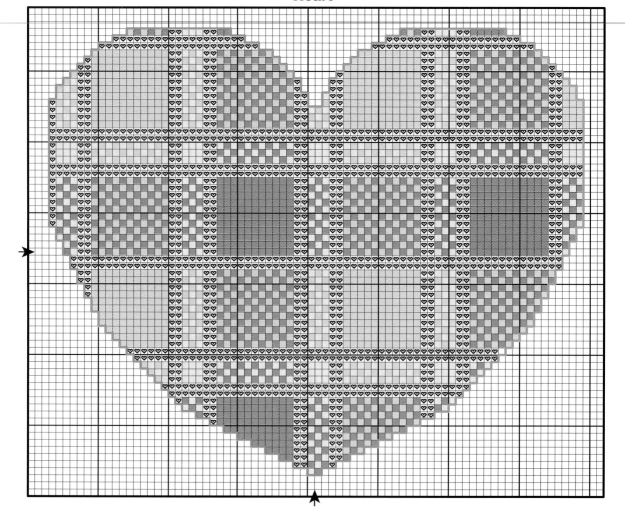

ring. Press under ½" along long edges of 2" x 90" bias strip. Fold in half lengthwise with wrong sides together; press. Encase one long edge of fabric ring with bias strip as shown in photo.

4: Gather unfinished edge of fabric ring to fit around pillow front; baste in place. With right sides together and with ½" seam, stitch front and back together, being careful not to catch outside edge of ruffle in seam and leaving an opening; trim seam. Turn right side out; press. Fill with fiberfill and slip stitch opening closed.❖

Heart
Stitch Count:
76 wide x 63 high

Approximate
Design Size:
11-count 7" x 5¾"
14-count 5½" x 4½"
16-count 4¾" x 4"
18-count 4¼" x 3½"
22-count 3½" x 2⅞"

X	B'st	DMC	ANCHOR	J.&P. COATS	COLORS
■	✎	#322	#978	#7978	Navy Blue Very Lt.
☐		#744	#301	#2293	Yellow Dark
☐		#745	#300	#2296	Yellow Pale
▨		#957	#50	#3125	Pink Med.
▨		#963	#73	#3173	Antique Rose Lt.
▨		#3325	#129	#7976	Baby Blue
♡		White	#2	#1001	White

Horse
Stitch Count:
80 wide x 79 high

Approximate
Design Size:
11-count 7⅜" x 7¼"
14-count 5¾" x 5¾"
16-count 5" x 5"
18-count 4½" x 4⅜"
22-count 3⅝" x 3⅝"

Horse

Tiny Touches

Share your warm-hearted
thoughts by giving the perfect
little gift. Whether
for Mother's Day, a
housewarming, or the
birthday of your best friend,
the extra touch of your
favorite needlework motif will
be a delight for many years
to come ...
each stitch a memory of
kindness expressed with
needle and thread.

Flower Baskets

Instructions on next page

113

Flower Baskets

DESIGNED BY JUDY CHRISPENS

MATERIALS:

Four 8" x 8" pieces of ivory 14-count Aida; 4⅞" x 20" wooden frame with 3" openings; Foam core board; Polyester batting; Craft glue or glue gun

INSTRUCTIONS:

1: Center and stitch one design onto each piece of Aida, using two strands floss for Cross Stitch and French Knots of pink flowers. Use one strand floss for Backstitch.

NOTE: From foam core board, cut four circles to fit frame openings.

2: Trim batting to fit boards. Center one stitched Aida piece on top of one board. Trim Aida edges to 1" larger than board; fold edges back and glue to secure. Repeat with remaining three stitched Aida pieces. Position and secure each mounted Aida into frame openings.❖

Yellow Flowers
Stitch Count:
39 wide x 31 high

Approximate Design Size:
11-count 3⅝" x 2⅞"
14-count 2⅞" x 2¼"
16-count 2½" x 2"
18-count 2¼" x 1¾"
22-count 1⅞" x 1½"

X	B'st	DMC	ANCHOR	JPC	COLORS
Yellow Flowers					
D		#722	#323	#2306	Golden Brown
☐		#725	#305	#2298	Canary Deep
		#746	#275	#1002	Off White
▲		#780	#365	#5000	Russet
	✎	#938	#381	#5477	Coffee Brown Ultra Dk.
■		#975	#357	#5349	Golden Brown Dk.
+		#977	#363	#2306	Golden Brown
		#986	#246	#6021	Pistachio Green Ultra Dk.
O		#987	#244	#6258	Willow Green
		#989	#242	#6266	Apple Green
≥		#3078	#292	#2292	Golden Yellow Very Lt.
		#3341	#328	#3008	Peach Flesh

Yellow Flowers

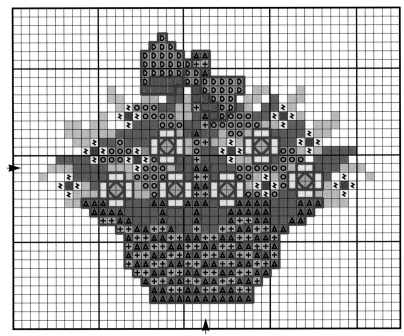

Red Flowers
Stitch Count:
31 wide x 30 high

Approximate Design Size:
11-count 2⅞" x 2¾"
14-count 2¼" x 2¼"
16-count 2" x 1⅞"
18-count 1¾" x 1¾"
22-count 1½" x 1⅜"

Red Flowers

X	B'st	DMC	ANCHOR	JPC	COLORS
▨		#304	#19	#3401	Rose Ultra Deep
▨		#435	#369	#5371	Topaz Very Ultra Dk.
		#437	#368	#5942	Tan Brown Lt.
▪		#666	#46	#3046	Christmas Red Bright
V		#745	#300	#2296	Yellow Pale
▪		#816	#20	#3410	Christmas Red Very Dk.
▪		#905	#258	#6267	Avocado Green
O		#906	#256	#6256	Parrot Green Med.
		#907	#255	#6001	Parrot Green Lt.
	╱	#938	#381	#5477	Coffee Brown Ultra Dk.

Red Flowers

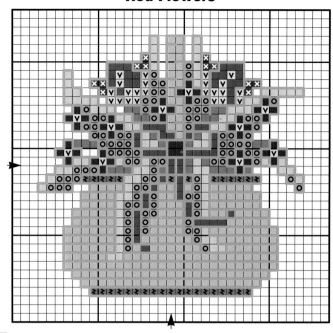

Blue Flowers
Stitch Count:
30 wide x 28 high

Approximate Design Size:
11-count 2¾" x 2⅝"
14-count 2¼" x 2"
16-count 1⅞" x 1¾"
18-count 1¾" x 1⅝"
22-count 1⅜" x 1⅜"

Blue Flowers

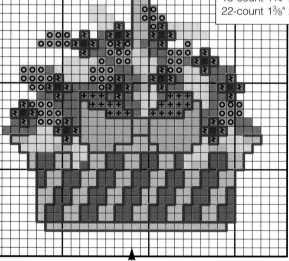

Blue Flowers

X	B'st	DMC	ANCHOR	JPC	COLORS
▨		#322	#978	#7978	Navy Blue Very Lt.
▪		#433	#358	#5471	Coffee Brown
		#772	#260	#6250	Pine Green Lt.
▪		#823	#149	#7982	Navy Blue Very Dk.
	╱	#938	#381	#5477	Coffee Brown Ultra Dk.
✚		#961	#76	#3153	Geranium
		#3032	#903	#5393	Beige Grey Very Dk.
		#3354	#74	#3003	Dusty Rose Lt.
		#3363	#262	#6317	Pine Green Med.
O		#3364	#261	#6010	Avocado Green Lt.

Pink Flowers

X	B'st	Fr	DMC	ANCHOR	JPC	COLORS
▪			#315	#972	#3082	Antique Mauve Dk.
			#320	#215	#6017	Pistachio Green Med.
▪			#367	#217	#6018	Pistachio Green Dk.
▪			#433	#310	#5471	Coffee Brown
			#435	#901	#5371	Topaz Very Ultra Dk.
		◉	#746	#275	#1002	Off White
▨			#902	#72	#3083	Garnet Very Dk.
	╱		#938	#381	#5477	Coffee Brown Ultra Dk.
			#3713	#968	#3068	Salmon Lt.
O			#3731	#77	#3283	Rose

Pink Flowers
Stitch Count:
34 wide x 27 high

Approximate Design Size:
11-count 3⅛" x 2½"
14-count 2½" x 2"
16-count 2⅛" x 1¾"
18-count 2" x 1½"
22-count 1⅝" x 1¼"

Pink Flowers

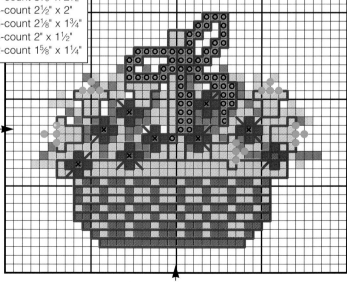

Delicate Florals

DESIGNED BY KATHLEEN HURLEY

MATERIALS:

Three 8" x 9" pieces of white 11-count Aida; ¼ yd. each of yellow, green and pink gingham; ¼ yd. white fabric; ¼ yd. crisp iron-on backing material; ⅝ yd. each of yellow and pink narrow piping; Wide yellow bias tape; 1¼ yds. white ⅝" eyelet; ⅜ yd. white 1" eyelet with beading; ⅜ yd. pink ⅜" grosgrain ribbon; 1⅛ yds. white narrow satin cording; 4" diameter chipwood box; Thin cardboard; Polyester fiberfill or potpourri; Quilt batting; Craft glue or glue gun

INSTRUCTIONS:

1: Center and stitch one design onto each piece of Aida, using three strands floss for Cross Stitch and one strand floss for Backstitch. Use one strand floss for French Knots of Daffodil and Fuchsia.

Sachet Pillow

NOTES: Trim stitched Magnolia to 5" wide x 5¾" tall for front. From green gingham, cut one 5" x 5¾" piece for back and one 2" x 40" strip for ruffle.

1: For ruffle, with right sides together and with ¼" seam, stitch short edges of gingham strip together, forming ring. Repeat with ⅝" eyelet, forming ring. Fold gingham ring in half lengthwise with wrong sides together; press. Place eyelet ring on top of gingham ring with unfinished edges even, run two rows of gathering threads along unfinished edges; pull gathers to fit outside edge of stitched front.

2: Pin and baste in place to front, first pink piping, then ruffle. With right sides together and with ¼" seams, stitch front and back together, being careful not to stitch outside edge of ruffle in seam and leaving an opening for turning; trim and clip seams. Turn right sides out; fill with fiberfill or potpourri. Slip stitch opening closed.

Dresser Box

1: Cut thin cardboard to fit top of box lid; cut craft batting same size. Center stitched Fuchsia on top of batting and cardboard with right side facing out. Trim Aida edges to 1½" larger than cardboard; fold edges back and glue to secure. Glue on top of lid.

2: Weave pink ⅜" grosgrain ribbon through eyelet beading. Glue onto lid lip as shown in photo.

3: Cut and glue pink gingham to fit around box as shown.

Mini Tote

NOTES: Trim stitched Daffodil to 6½" wide x 7½" tall. From yellow gingham, cut one 6½" x 7½" piece for back, two 2¼" x 7½" pieces for sides, one 2¼" x 6½" piece for bottom and one 2½" x 12" bias strip for top ruffle. From white fabric, cut two 6½" x 7½" pieces for front and back lining, two 2½" x 7½" pieces for side linings and one 2¼" x 6½" piece for bottom lining. From backing material, cut pieces same as front, back sides and bottom.

1: Iron backing material pieces to wrong sides of front, back, sides and bottom. Sew yellow piping around front, sides and bottom as shown in photo.

2: With right sides together and with ¼" seams, sew front, back and side pieces together at side seams. With right sides together and with ¼" seams, sew bottom to bottom opening of Tote; turn right sides out. Repeat with lining pieces, omitting backing material.

3: With wrong sides together, place lining inside Tote; baste top edges together. Fold bias strip ruffle in half lengthwise with right sides together; with ¼" seams, stitch short ends. Turn right side out; press. Gather ruffle to fit top front of Tote; baste in place.

4: With right sides together and with ½" seams, stitch yellow bias tape around tope edge of Tote. Fold bias tape over top edge and slip stitch in place. Cut white satin cording into three equal pieces. Braid pieces, forming handle. Sew handle to Tote sides.❖

Daffodil

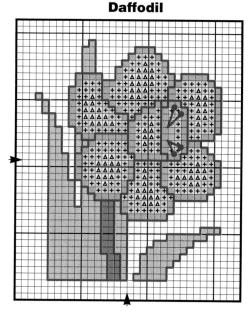

X	B'st	Fr	DMC	ANCHOR	JPC	COLORS
◪			#209	#109	#4302	Lavender Med. Lt.
	╱	●	#310	#403	#8403	Black
◎			#603	#62	#3001	Cranberry Lt.
+			#726	#295	#2294	Topaz Lt.
			#743	#302	#2302	Orange Lt.
			#905	#258	#6267	Avocado Green
			#961	#76	#3153	Geranium
			#989	#242	#6266	Apple Green
△			#3078	#292	#2292	Golden Yellow Very Lt.
			#3354	#74	#3003	Dusty Rose Lt.
			#3371	#382	#5478	Brown Very Ultra Dk.

Magnolia

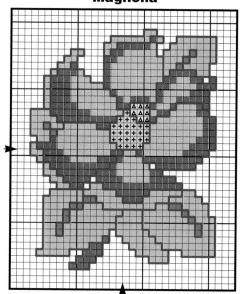

Magnolia & Daffodil Stitch Count:
28 wide x 36 high

Approximate Design Size:
11-count 2⅝" x 3⅜"
14-count 2" x 2⅝"
16-count 1¾" x 2¼"
18-count 1⅝" x 2"
22-count 1⅜" x 1⅝"

Fuchsia Stitch Count:
28 wide x 35 high

Approximate Design Size:
11-count 2⅝" x 3¼"
14-count 2" x 2½"
16-count 1¾" x 2¼"
18-count 1⅝" x 2"
22-count 1⅜" x 1⅝"

Fuchsia

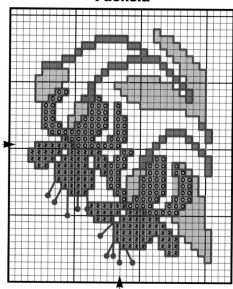

Mini Gift Bags

DESIGNED BY JUDY CHRISPENS

MATERIALS:

Four 8½" x 8½" pieces of sesame 14-count Aida; Two 8" x 8" pieces of Tucson tan 14-count Aida; ⅛ yd. of 45" fabric; ½ yd. of ¾" flat lace; ⅝ yd. of 1" satin ribbon; ½ yd. of ¼" satin ribbon, picot satin ribbon and grosgrain ribbon; Craft glue or glue gun

INSTRUCTIONS:

1: Center and stitch Bath Salts and Nouveau Tulip designs each onto one piece of sesame Aida and Tea Bags design onto one piece of Tucson tan Aida, using three strands floss for Cross Stitch and two strands floss for Backstitch.

2: For bag fronts and backs, cut stitched and unstitched pieces into 4½" x 5½" rectangles, cutting bottom corners diagonally.

3: With right sides together and with ¼" seams, sew fronts and backs together; trim seams and turn right sides out. Narrowly zigzag and hem top edges.

4: For Nouveau Tulip, cut one 3" x 20" piece of fabric. Sew short ends together, forming ring. Fold fabric in half lengthwise; press. Pleat fabric to fit bag opening. For Tea Bags, sew short ends of 1" satin ribbon together, forming ring. Pleat ribbon to fit bag opening. For Bath Salts, sew short ends of lace together, forming ring. Pull gathers to fit bag opening.

5: Glue ruffle to inside top edges of each bag. Using ribbon as shown in photo, glue ribbon and bow to top edge of each bag. ❖

Tea Bags

X	B'st	DMC	ANCHOR	JPC	COLOR
		#502	#877	#6876	Blue Green
		#561	#212	#6211	Jade Very Dk.
		#726	#295	#2294	Topaz Lt.
	✎	#815	#44	#3000	Garnet
	✎	#890	#246	#6021	Pistachio Green Ultra Dk.
		White	#2	#1001	White

Tea Bags Stitch Count:
34 wide x 31 high

Approximate Design Size:
11-count 4⅛" x 3½"
14-count 3¼" x 2¾"
16-count 2⅞" x 2⅜"
18-count 2½" x 2⅛"
22-count 2⅛" x 1¾"

Nouveau Tulip

X	DMC	ANCHOR	JPC	COLOR
	#351	#10	#3011	Coral
	#352	#9	#3008	Peach Flesh
	#353	#8	#3006	Peach Flesh Lt.
	#435	#901	#5371	Topaz Very Ultra Dk.
	#502	#877	#6876	Blue Green
	#561	#212	#6211	Jade Very Dk.
	#796	#133	#7100	Royal Blue Dk.
	#798	#131	#7022	Cornflower Blue Dk.
	#890	#246	#6021	Pistachio Green Ultra Dk.

Tea Bags

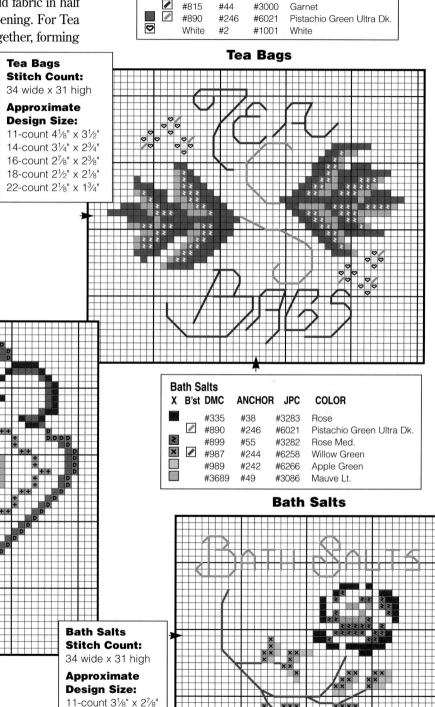

Bath Salts

X	B'st	DMC	ANCHOR	JPC	COLOR
		#335	#38	#3283	Rose
	✎	#890	#246	#6021	Pistachio Green Ultra Dk.
		#899	#55	#3282	Rose Med.
	✎	#987	#244	#6258	Willow Green
		#989	#242	#6266	Apple Green
		#3689	#49	#3086	Mauve Lt.

Bath Salts

Nouveau Tulip

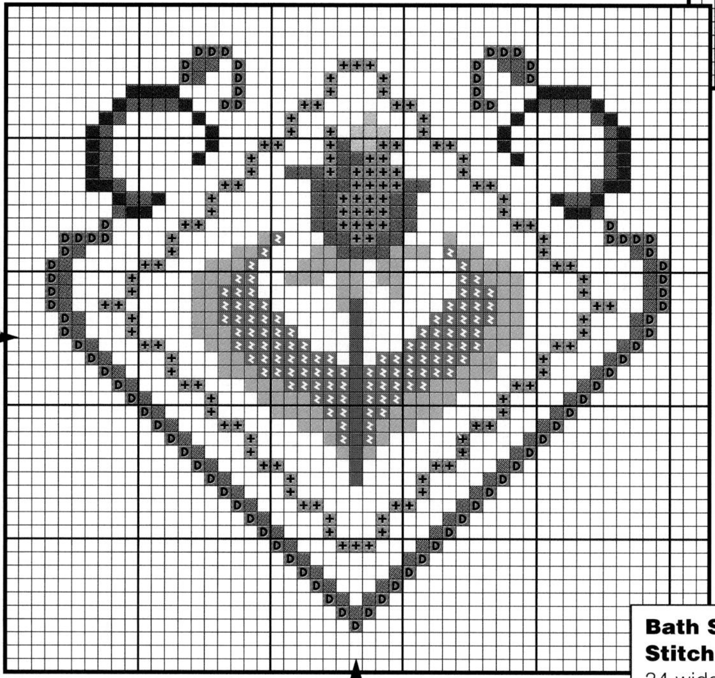

Nouveau Tulip Stitch Count:
34 wide x 31 high

Approximate Design Size:
11-count 4⅜" x 4"
14-count 3⅜" x 3¼"
16-count 3" x 2¾"
18-count 2⅝" x 2½"
22-count 2⅛" x 2"

Bath Salts Stitch Count:
34 wide x 31 high

Approximate Design Size:
11-count 3⅛" x 2⅞"
14-count 2½" x 2¼"
16-count 2⅛" x 2"
18-count 2" x 1¾"
22-count 1⅝" x 1½"

Just for You

Designed by Virginia G. Soskin

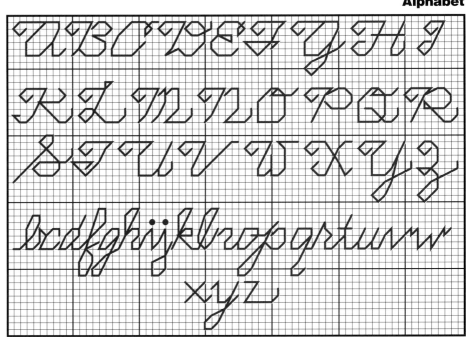

MATERIALS:

Two 8" x 9" pieces of antique white 14-count Aida; 4" x 4" piece of white 14-count perforated paper; ¼ yd. of white ½" pre-gathered lace; ½ yd. of ¼" satin ribbon; Craft glue or glue gun

INSTRUCTIONS:

Favor Bag

1: Count down 30 squares from one short edge of one piece of Aida; begin top of design. Stitch Favor Bag design, using two strands floss for Cross Stitch, French Knots, Eyelet Stitch and Backstitch.

2: For bag front and back,

cut stitched and unstitched pieces into 5" x 6½" rectangles. With right sides together and with ¼" seams, sew front and back together at sides and bottom; trim seams and turn right sides out. Narrowly zigzag and hem top edges.

3: Sew short ends of lace together forming ring to fit bag opening. Glue ruffle to inside top edge of bag. Wrap ribbon around bag and tie into a bow as shown in photo.

Place Card

1: Choosing letters from Alphabet graph, center and stitch Place Card design onto perforated paper. Use two strands floss for Cross Stitch, Eyelet Stitch, French Knots and Backstitch.

2: Carefully cut around top of design as indicated; fold card on fold line. ❖

Place Card
Stitch Count:
49 wide x 36 high

Approximate Design Size:
11-count 4½" x 3⅜"
14-count 3½" x 2⅝"
16-count 3⅛" x 2¼"
18-count 2¾" x 2"
22-count 2¼" x 1⅝"

Favor Bag
Stitch Count:
38 wide x 46 high

Approximate Design Size:
11-count 3½" x 4¼"
14-count 2¾" x 3⅜"
16-count 2⅜" x 2⅞"
18-count 2⅛" x 2⅝"
22-count 1¾" x 2⅛"

Place Card

	Cutting Line
- - - -	Folding Line

Place Card

X	B'st	Fr	Eye	DMC	ANCHOR	JPC	COLORS
	▨			#208	#110	#4301	Lavender Med.
■				#209	#109	#4302	Lavender Med. Lt.
+				#210	#108	#4303	Lavender Lt.
▨			▨	#519	#168	#7159	Blue Very Lt.
□		□		#744	#301	#2293	Yellow Dark
✕				#747	#928	#7053	Larkspur Lt.
▣			▨	#813	#160	#7161	Blue Lt.
▧				#3045	#888	#2412	Mustard
▨				#3347	#266	#6267	Avocado Green
D			▨	#3348	#254	#6266	Apple Green
▨				#3363	#262	#6317	Pine Green Med.
◖				#3607	#87	#3088	Mauve
▲				#3608	#86	#3087	Mauve Med.
▨				#3609	#85	#3086	Mauve Lt.
	▨	●		#3787	#393	#5393	Beige Grey Very Dk.

Favor Bag							
X	B'st	Fr	Eye	DMC	ANCHOR	JPC	COLORS
				#208	#110	#4301	Lavender Med.
				#209	#109	#4302	Lavender Med. Lt.
				#210	#108	#4303	Lavender Lt.
	▨		▨	#519	#168	#7159	Blue Very Lt.
				#744	#301	#2293	Yellow Dark
				#747	#928	#7053	Larkspur Lt.
				#813	#160	#7161	Blue Lt.
		□		#3045	#888	#2412	Mustard
				#3347	#266	#6267	Avocado Green
				#3348	#254	#6266	Apple Green
	▨			#3363	#262	#6317	Pine Green Med.
				#3607	#87	#3088	Mauve
				#3608	#86	#3087	Mauve Med.
				#3609	#85	#3086	Mauve Lt.
	▨	●		#3787	#393	#5393	Beige Grey Very Dk.

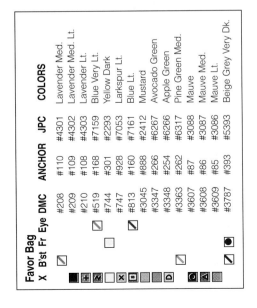

Favor Bag

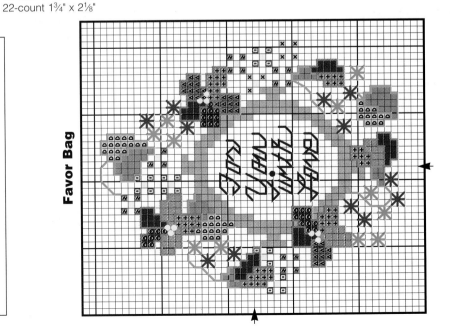

Early Spring Irises

DESIGNED BY BONNIE CRAWFORD

MATERIALS:

8" x 10" piece of white 14-count Aida; One 6¾" length of 1⅞" white 16-count cross stitch ribbon; ⅓ yd. of piping; ⅝ yd. of white ½" flat trim; Blue fabric eyeglass case

INSTRUCTIONS:

1: For Bookmark, center and stitch design onto cross stitch ribbon, using two strands floss for Cross Stitch and one strand floss for Backstitch. To fray ends, pull ½" crosswise threads out of each end; with blunt end of needle, separate lengthwise threads.

2: For Eyeglass Case, center and stitch design onto Aida, using two strands floss for Cross Stitch and one strand floss for Backstitch.

3: Trim stitched Aida into oval slightly larger than stitched design and leaving ½" seam allowance. With right sides together and with ½" seams, sew piping around stitched Aida. Press seams to wrong side. Slip stitch flat trim around outside edge under piping. Slip stitch finished piece to front of eyeglass case and flat trim to opening.❖

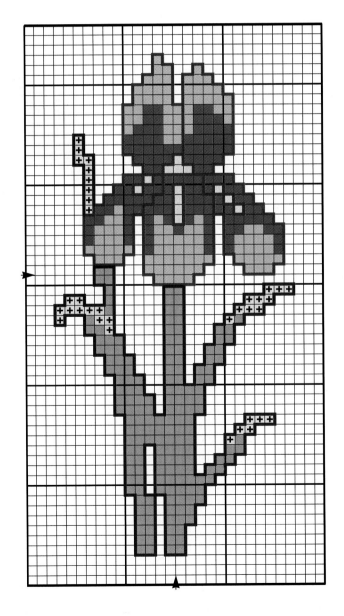

X	B'st	DMC	ANCHOR	JPC	COLORS
	∕	#319	#218	#6246	Pistachio Green Very Dk.
		#320	#215	#6017	Pistachio Green Med.
+		#504	#213	#6875	Blue Green Lt.
		#743	#302	#2302	Orange Lt.
	∕	#791	#178	#7024	Royal Blue Very Dk.
		#792	#177	#7150	Cornflower Blue Very Dk.
		#794	#175	#7977	Baby Blue Med.

Stitch Count:
24 wide x 50 high

Approximate Design Size:
11-count 2¼" x 4⅝"
14-count 1¾" x 3⅝"
16-count 1½" x 3⅛"
18-count 1⅜" x 2⅞"
22-count 1⅛" x 2⅜"

Filigree Linens

Instructions on next page

Filigree Linens

DESIGNED BY C.M. BARR

MATERIALS FOR SET:

Ivory 14-count place mat, napkin and bread cloth

using two strands floss for Cross Stitch and one strand floss for Backstitch.❖

INSTRUCTIONS:

1: Stitch border design on one short end of place mat, starting design nine squares from outside edges and using two strands floss for Cross Stitch and one strand floss for Backstitch. Repeat design across as shown in photo.

2: Stitch corner design on one corner of napkin and bread cloth, starting design seven squares from outside edges and

Corner Design Stitch Count:
33 wide x 33 high

Approximate Design Size:
11-count 3" x 3"
14-count 2⅜" x 2⅜"
16-count 2⅛" x 2⅛"
18-count 1⅞" x 1⅞"
22-count 1½" x 1½"

X	B'st	DMC	ANCHOR	JPC	COLOR
		#315	#972	#3082	Antique Mauve Dk.
		#316	#969	#3081	Antique Mauve Med.
		#729	#874	#5363	Old Gold Lt.
	✎	#924	#851	#6008	Green Mist Dk.
		#926	#850	#6007	Green Mist Med.
		#3053	#858	#6315	Fern Green Very Lt.

Corner

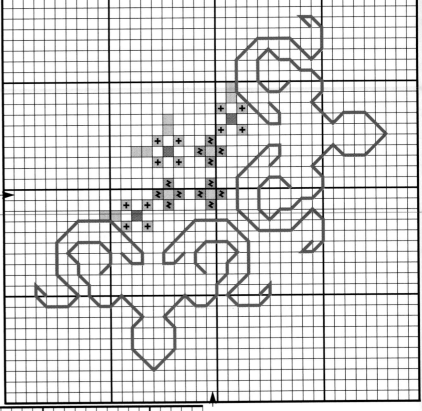

Border

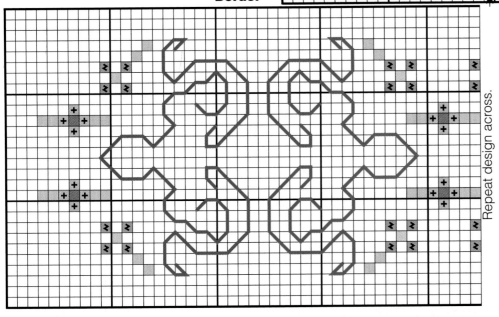

Repeat design across.

Border Design Stitch Count:
147 wide x 22 high

Approximate Design Size:
11-count 13⅜" x 2"
14-count 10½" x 1⅝"
16-count 9¼" x 1⅜"
18-count 8¼" x 1¼"
22-count 6¾" x 1"

Sweet Scents

TAKE TIME
TO SMELL

THE
FLOWERS

Instructions on next page

Sweet Scents

Designed by Carole Rodgers

MATERIALS:

12" x 12" piece of white 14-count Aida; ¼ yd. of white ¾" pre-gathered eyelet ; Thread

INSTRUCTIONS:

1: Center and stitch design, using two strands floss for Cross Stitch and one strand floss for Backstitch.

Bottom Pattern

NOTE: Trim stitched Aida to 6½" tall x 7½" wide; cut bottom from remaining Aida, following Bottom Pattern.

2: With right sides together and with ½" seam, stitch side seam; press open. With right sides together and with ¼" seam, stitch bottom to bottom opening of cover. Press under ½" on top edge of cover; finish edge. Stitch eyelet to top inside edge.❖

Stitch Count:
39 wide x 48 high

Approximate Design Size:
11-count 3⅝"x 4⅜"
14-count 2⅞" x 3½"
16-count 2½" x 3"
18-count 2¼"x 2¾"
22-count 1⅞" x 2¼"

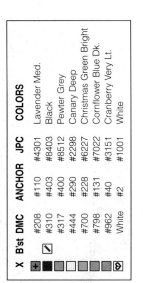

X	B'st	DMC	ANCHOR	JPC	COLORS
		#208	#110	#4301	Lavender Med.
		#310	#403	#8403	Black
		#317	#400	#8512	Pewter Grey
		#444	#290	#2298	Canary Deep
		#700	#228	#6227	Christmas Green Bright
		#798	#131	#7022	Cornflower Blue Dk.
		#962	#40	#3151	Cranberry Very Lt.
		White	#2	#1001	White

Bed & Bath

Instructions on next page

Bed & Bath

DESIGNED BY CAROLE RODGERS

MATERIALS FOR ONE;

6" x 6" piece of pink 14-count Aida; 1 yd. pink ⅛" satin ribbon; ¼ yd. white 1" pre-gathered lace; Cardboard; Polyester batting; Craft glue or glue gun

INSTRUCTIONS:

Bubble Bath

1: Center and stitch design, using two strands floss for Cross Stitch. Use two strands floss for Backstitch of lettering and one strand floss for remaining Backstitch.

Hearts

1: Center and stitch design, using two strands floss for Cross Stitch.

Potpourri

1: Center and stitch design, using two strands floss for Cross Stitch. Use two strands floss for Backstitch of lettering and one strand floss for remaining Backstitch.

LID INSTRUCTIONS;

1: Cut cardboard to fit lid. Trim stitched Aida and batting 1" larger than cardboard. With right side facing up, center stitched design over cardboard; fold outside edges to back of cardboard and glue to secure.

2: Whipstitch lace and blue ribbon around outside edges.❖

Bubble Bath

X	B'st	JPC(SS)	DMC	ANCHOR	J.&P. COATS	COLORS
●		#1	White	#2	#1001	White
◎	✎	#12	#310	#403	#8403	Black
		#30	#898	#360	#5476	Dk. Brown
		#40	#415	#398	#8510	Silver
		#60	#783	#307	#2307	Gold
	✎	#75	#961	#76	#3153	Rose
		#84	#809	#130	#7021	Lt. Royal Blue

Bubble Bath

Bubble Bath Stitch Count:
29 wide x 33 high

Approximate Design Size:
11-count 2⅝" x 3"
14-count 2⅛" x 2⅜"
16-count 1⅞" x 2⅛"
18-count 1⅝" x 1⅞"
22-count 1⅜" x 1½"

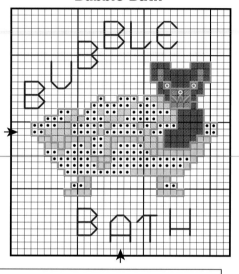

Potpourri

X	B'st	JPC(SS)	DMC	ANCHOR	J.&P. COATS	COLORS
		#21	#727	#293	#2289	Canary Yellow
	✎	#30	#898	#360	#5476	Dk. Brown
		#65	#910	#229	#6031	Green
		#70	#3716	#25	#3150	Pink
	✎	#75	#961	#76	#3153	Rose
		#84	#809	#130	#7021	Lt. Royal Blue
	✎	#85	#797	#132	#7023	Royal Blue

Potpourri Stitch Count:
26 wide x 29 high

Approximate Design Size:
11-count 2⅜" x 2⅝"
14-count 1⅞" x 2⅛"
16-count 1⅝" x 1⅞"
18-count 1½" x 1⅝"
22-count 1¼" x 1⅜"

Potpourri

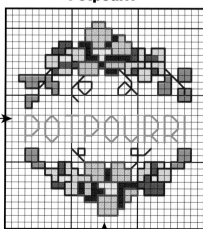

Hearts Stitch Count:
29 wide x 29 high

Approximate Design Size:
11-count 2⅝" x 2⅝"
14-count 2⅛" x 2⅛"
16-count 1⅞" x 1⅞"
18-count 1⅝" x 1⅝"
22-count 1⅜" x 1⅜"

Hearts

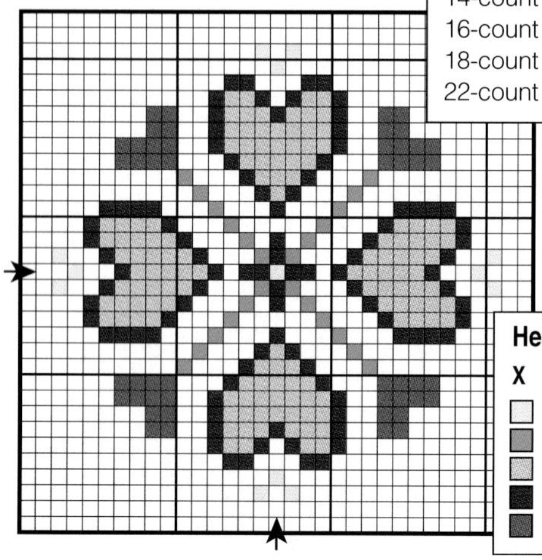

Hearts

X	JPC(SS)	DMC	ANCHOR	J.&P. COATS	COLORS
	#24	#726	#295	#2284	Yellow
	#65	#910	#229	#6031	Green
	#70	#3716	#25	#3150	Pink
	#75	#961	#76	#3153	Rose
	#85	#797	#132	#7023	Royal Blue

Words of Wisdom

*Celebrate the inspirations
found in scripture and the
serenity found in nature.
Whether you choose a frame,
pillow or tote bag as your
finishing touch, cross stitch
captures the thought for
generations to come …
each and every loving stitch
a blessing bestowed and
a prayer of peace sent
heavenward in joy
and gratitude.*

Instructions on next page

Nature's Grandeur

DESIGNED BY CAROLE RODGERS

MATERIALS:

One 13" x 15" and two 10" x 12" pieces of ice blue 28-count Annabelle

INSTRUCTIONS:

1: Center and stitch God's Hand design onto 13" x 15" piece of Annabelle and Mountain Hideaway and Secluded Lake designs onto 10" x 12" pieces of Annabelle, stitching over two threads and using two strands floss for Cross Stitch and one strand floss for Backstitch and French Knots.❖

Graphs continued on page 136

Mountain Hideaway
Stitch Count:
56 wide x 80 high

Approximate Design Size:
11-count 5⅛" x 7⅜"
14-count 4" x 5¾"
16-count 3½" x 5"
18-count 3⅛" x 4½"
22-count 2⅝" x 3⅝"
28-count over two threads 4" x 5¾"

Mountain Hideaway

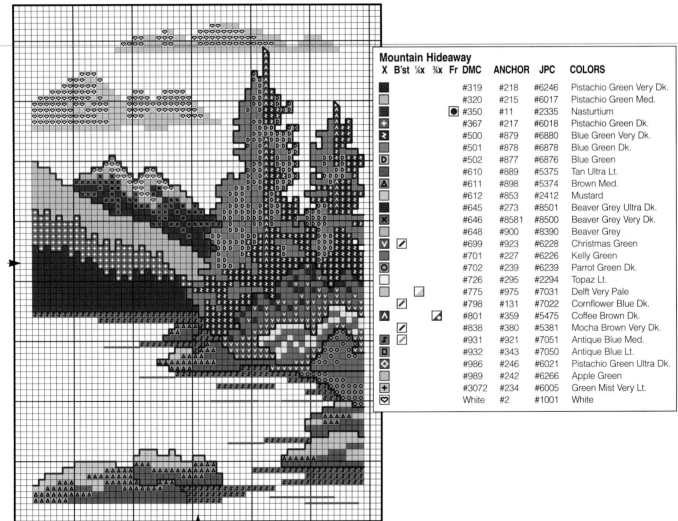

X	B'st	¼x	¾x	Fr	DMC	ANCHOR	JPC	COLORS
					#319	#218	#6246	Pistachio Green Very Dk.
					#320	#215	#6017	Pistachio Green Med.
				●	#350	#11	#2335	Nasturtium
					#367	#217	#6018	Pistachio Green Dk.
					#500	#879	#6880	Blue Green Very Dk.
					#501	#878	#6878	Blue Green Dk.
					#502	#877	#6876	Blue Green
					#610	#889	#5375	Tan Ultra Lt.
					#611	#898	#5374	Brown Med.
					#612	#853	#2412	Mustard
					#645	#273	#8501	Beaver Grey Ultra Dk.
					#646	#8581	#8500	Beaver Grey Very Dk.
					#648	#900	#8390	Beaver Grey
	✓				#699	#923	#6228	Christmas Green
					#701	#227	#6226	Kelly Green
					#702	#239	#6239	Parrot Green Dk.
					#726	#295	#2294	Topaz Lt.
			◩		#775	#975	#7031	Delft Very Pale
	✓				#798	#131	#7022	Cornflower Blue Dk.
			◩		#801	#359	#5475	Coffee Brown Dk.
	✓				#838	#380	#5381	Mocha Brown Very Dk.
	✓				#931	#921	#7051	Antique Blue Med.
					#932	#343	#7050	Antique Blue Lt.
					#986	#246	#6021	Pistachio Green Ultra Dk.
					#989	#242	#6266	Apple Green
					#3072	#234	#6005	Green Mist Very Lt.
					White	#2	#1001	White

God's Hand

God's Hand
Stitch Count:
126 wide x 95 high

Approximate Design Size:
11-count 11½" x 8⅝"
14-count 9" x 6⅞"
16-count 7⅞" x 6"
18-count 7" x 5⅜"
22-count 5¾" x 4⅜"
28-count over two
threads 9" x 6⅞"

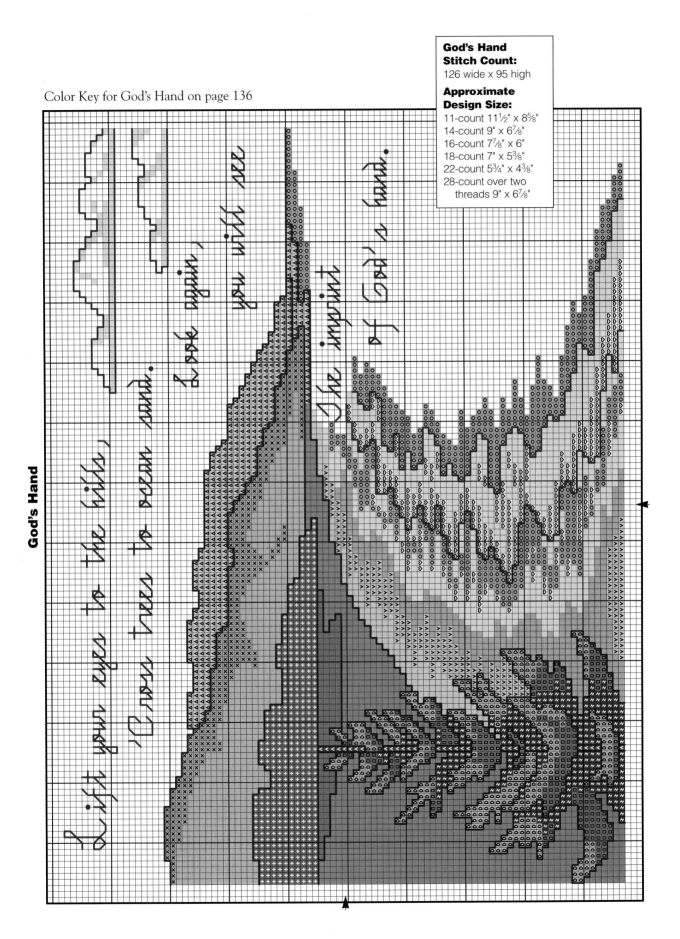

Secluded Lake

**Secluded Lake
Stitch Count:**
56 wide x 84 high

**Approximate
Design Size:**
11-count 5⅛" x 7⅝"
14-count 4" x 6"
16-count 3½" x 5¼"
18-count 3⅛" x 4¾"
22-count 2⅝" x 3⅞"
28-count over two
  threads 4" x 6"

Secluded Lake

X	B'st	¼x	¾x	Fr	DMC	ANCHOR	JPC	COLORS
					#319	#218	#6246	Pistachio Green Very Dk.
					#320	#215	#6017	Pistachio Green Med.
				●	#350	#11	#2335	Nasturtium
					#367	#217	#6018	Pistachio Green Dk.
					#500	#879	#6880	Blue Green Very Dk.
					#501	#878	#6878	Blue Green Dk.
					#502	#877	#6876	Blue Green
					#610	#889	#5375	Tan Ultra Lt.
					#611	#898	#5374	Brown Med.
					#612	#853	#2412	Mustard
					#645	#273	#8501	Beaver Grey Ultra Dk.
					#646	#8581	#8500	Beaver Grey Very Dk.
					#648	#900	#8390	Beaver Grey
					#699	#923	#6228	Christmas Green
					#701	#227	#6226	Kelly Green
					#702	#239	#6239	Parrot Green Dk.
					#726	#295	#2294	Topaz Lt.
					#775	#975	#7031	Delft Very Pale
					#798	#131	#7022	Cornflower Blue Dk.
					#801	#359	#5475	Coffee Brown Dk.
					#838	#380	#5381	Mocha Brown Very Dk.
					#931	#921	#7051	Antique Blue Med.
					#932	#343	#7050	Antique Blue Lt.
					#986	#246	#6021	Pistachio Green Ultra Dk.
					#989	#242	#6266	Apple Green
					#3072	#234	#6005	Green Mist Very Lt.
					White	#2	#1001	White

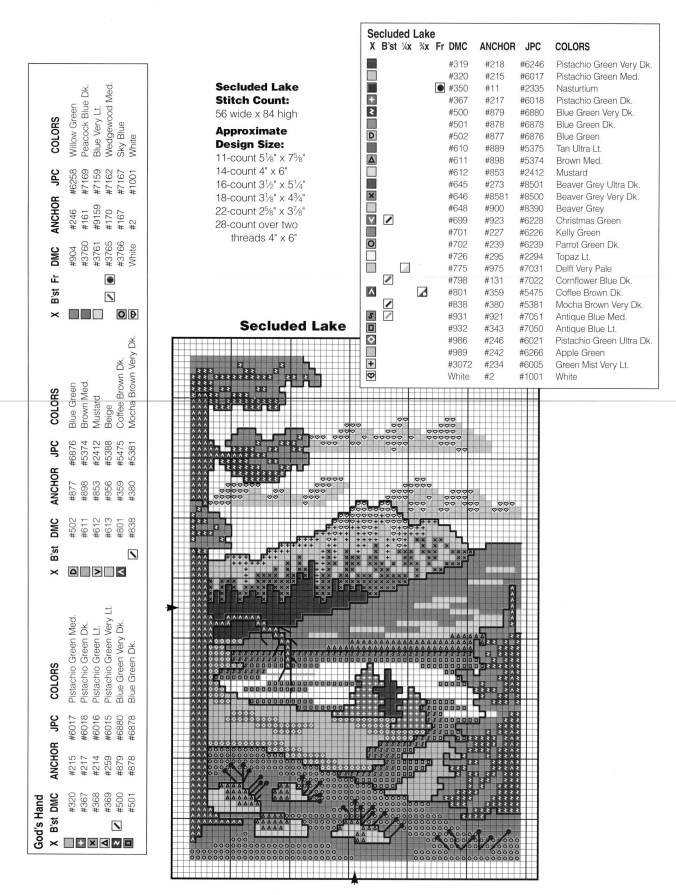

Secluded Lake

X	B'st	Fr	DMC	ANCHOR	JPC	COLORS
			#904	#246	#6258	Willow Green
			#3760	#161	#7169	Peacock Blue Dk.
			#3761	#9159	#7159	Blue Very Lt.
			#3765	#170	#7162	Wedgewood Med.
		●	#3766	#167	#7167	Sky Blue
			White	#2	#1001	White

God's Hand

X	B'st	DMC	ANCHOR	JPC	COLORS
		#320	#215	#6017	Pistachio Green Med.
		#367	#217	#6018	Pistachio Green Dk.
		#368	#214	#6016	Pistachio Green Lt.
		#369	#259	#6015	Pistachio Green Very Lt.
		#500	#879	#6880	Blue Green Very Dk.
		#501	#878	#6878	Blue Green Dk.

X	B'st	DMC	ANCHOR	JPC	COLORS
		#502	#877	#6876	Blue Green
		#611	#898	#5374	Brown Med.
		#612	#853	#2412	Mustard
		#613	#956	#5388	Beige
		#801	#359	#5475	Coffee Brown Dk.
		#838	#380	#5381	Mocha Brown Very Dk.

Serenity Prayer

Lord, grant me
the serenity to accept
the things I cannot
change, the courage
to change the things
I can and the wisdom
to know the
difference.

Instructions on next page

Serenity Prayer

DESIGNED BY KATHLEEN HURLEY

MATERIALS:

17" x 18" piece of white 25-count Dublin linen; Frame with 12⅜" x 14⅜" opening; Foam core board; Craft glue or glue gun

INSTRUCTIONS:

1: Center and stitch design, stitching over two theads and using two strands floss or one strand metallic braid for Cross Stitch. Use two strands floss for Backstitch of lettering and one strand floss or metallic braid for remaining Backstitch, Straight Stitch and French Knots.❖

Stitch Count:
128 wide x 141 high

Approximate Design Size:
11-count 11⅝" x 12⅞"
14-count 9¼" x 10⅛"
16-count 8" x 8⅞"
18-count 7⅛" x 7⅞"
22-count 5⅞" x 6½"
25-count over two
   threads 10¼" x 11⅜"

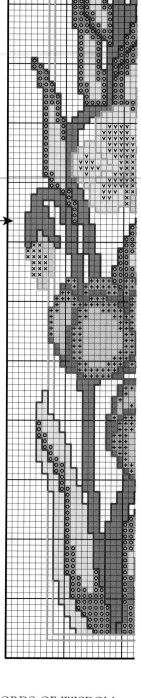

X	B'st	¼x	¾x	Fr	Str	DMC	ANCHOR	J.&P. COATS	COLORS	KREINIK(#8 MB)
▨						#209	#109	#4302	Lavender Med. Lt.	
▫						#211	#342	#4303	Lavender Lt.	
▨	◪	◪		●	◪	#309	#42	#3284	Rose Deep	
	◪					#310	#403	#8403	Black	
☒						#327	#100	#4101	Violet Dk.	
☑						#444	#290	#2290	Canary Bright	
▫						#746	#275	#2275	Lt. Cream	
	◪					#776	#24	#3281	Pink Med.	
	◪					#780	#310	#5000	Russet	
▨						#797	#132	#7143	Royal Blue Med.	
▫						#799	#136	#7030	Blue	
▫						#800	#144	#7020	Delft Pale	
➕						#899	#52	#3282	Rose Med.	
▫						#972	#298	#2298	Canary Deep	
▫						#3078	#292	#2292	Golden Yellow Very Lt.	
▨	◪					#3345	#268	#6258	Willow Green	
⊘						#3347	#266	#6010	Avocado Green Lt.	
▫						#3348	#264	#6266	Apple Green	
	◪					#3685	#1028	#3089	Mauve Dk.	
▨	▫		▫							#002 Gold

Lord, grant me
the serenity to accept
the things I cannot
change, the courage
to change the things
I can and the wisdom
to know the
difference.

Amazing Grace

DESIGNED BY VIRGINIA G. SOSKIN

MATERIALS:

16" x 19" piece of Fiddler's Lite® 14-count Aida; Frame with 12" x 15¼" opening; Foam core board; Craft glue or glue gun

INSTRUCTIONS:

NOTE: Double mat was professionally cut at a local frame shop.

1: Center and stitch design, stitching over two threads and using two strands floss for Cross Stitch. Use two strands floss for Backstitch and French Knots of music composition and lyrics. Use one strand floss for remaining Backstitch and French Knots.❖

Graph continued on next page

Stitch Count:
106 wide x 151 high

Approximate Design Size:
11-count 9⅝" x 13¾"
14-count 7⅝" x 10⅞"
16-count 6⅝" x 9½"
18-count 6" x 8⅜"
22-count 4⅞" x 6⅞"

X	B'st	¼x	Fr	DMC	ANCHOR	J&P. COATS	COLORS
				#316	#1017	#3081	Antique Mauve Med.
		●		#368	#214	#6016	Pistachio Green Lt.
				#434	#310	#5000	Russet
				#437	#362	#5942	Tan Brown Lt.
			●	#502	#877	#6876	Blue Green
				#676	#891	#2305	Wheat Straw
				#772	#259	#6250	Pine Green Lt.
				#800	#144	#7020	Delft Pale
				#801	#359	#5472	Coffee Brown Med.
				#963	#73	#3173	Antique Rose Lt.
				#3078	#292	#2292	Golden Yellow Very Lt.
				#3354	#74	#3003	Dusty Rose Lt.
				#3726	#1018	#3084	Antique Mauve
				#3755	#140	#7976	Baby Blue

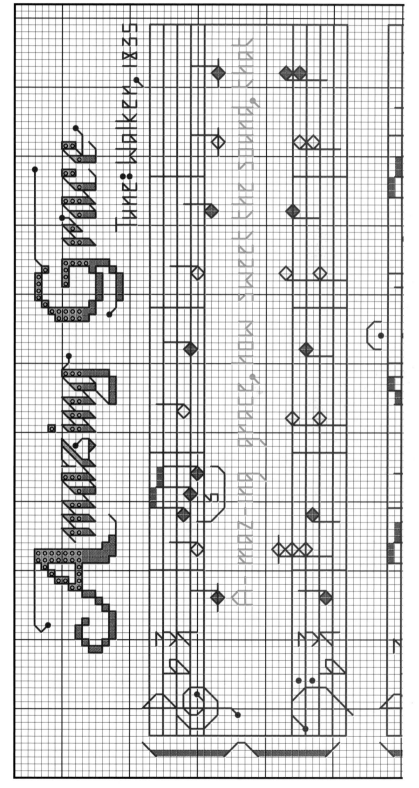

Graph continued from page 141

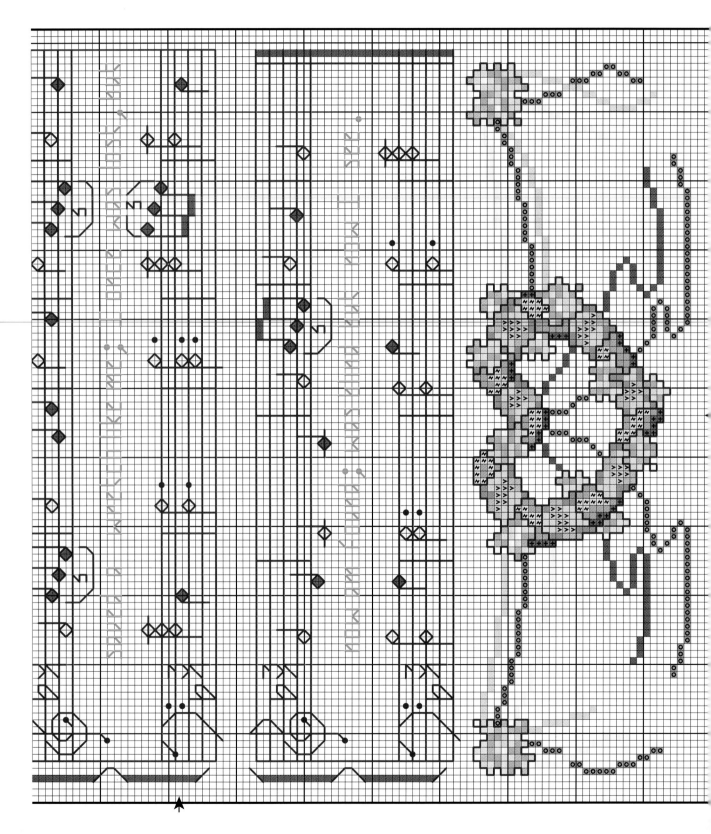

King of Kings

DESIGNED BY RITA BROOKS

MATERIALS:

15" x 17" piece of ivory 14-count Aida; ⅝ yd. 45" fabric; ⅝ yd. crisp iron-on backing material

INSTRUCTIONS:

1: Center and stitch design, using two strands floss for Cross Stitch and Backstitch.

NOTES: Trim stitched Aida to 11¾" wide x 10" tall for front. From fabric, cut three 11¾" x 10" pieces for back and front and back lining, four 4" x 10" pieces for sides and side linings, two 4" x 11¾" pieces for bottom and bottom lining, four 2½" x 14" pieces for handles and handle linings, two 4" x 6" pieces for side pockets and one 2" x 29" bias strip for top trim. From backing material, cut one front, one back, two sides, one bottom and two handles.

2: Iron corresponding backing material pieces to wrong sides of front, back, sides, bottom and handle pieces. Finish one short edge of each side pocket. Match unfinished short edge to bottom short edge of each side; baste in place. Stitch a seam lengthwise on pocket, dividing pocket into two sections, for holding pens.

3: With right sides together and with ½" seams, stitch front, back and side pieces together at side seams. Stay stitch ½" from bottom outside edges; clip corners. With right sides together and with ½" seams, stitch bottom to bottom opening of Tote. Turn right sides out. Repeat with lining pieces, omitting backing material. Do not turn right sides out.

4: With wrong sides together, place lining inside Tote;

Continued on next page

King of Kings

Continued from page 143

baste top edges together. With right sides together and with ½" seams, stitch handle and lining pieces together at long edges. Turn right sides out; press.

5: Position one handle to front and one handle to back at top edges; baste in place. With right sides together and with ½" seam, stitch bias trim around top edge. Fold bias strip over top edge and press under ½" of unfinished edge; slip stitch in place. Fold up handles; slip stitch in place.❖

Stitch Count:
139 wide x 113 high

Approximate Design Size:
11-count 12⅝" x 10⅜"
14-count 10" x 8⅛"
16-count 8¾" x 7⅛"
18-count 7¾" x 6⅜"
22-count 6⅜" x 5⅛"

Continue border pattern across unseen areas.

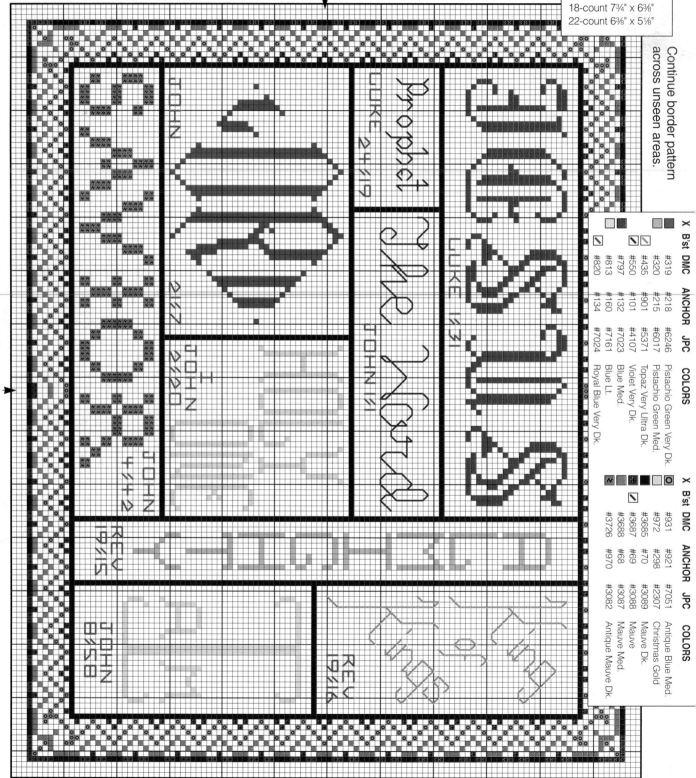

X	B'st	DMC	ANCHOR	JPC	COLORS
		#319	#218	#6246	Pistachio Green Very Dk.
		#320	#215	#6017	Pistachio Green Med.
		#435	#901	#5371	Topaz Very Ultra Dk.
		#550	#101	#4107	Violet Very Dk.
		#797	#132	#7023	Blue Med.
		#813	#160	#7161	Blue Lt.
		#820	#134	#7024	Royal Blue Very Dk.

X	B'st	DMC	ANCHOR	JPC	COLORS
		#931	#921	#7051	Antique Blue Med.
		#972	#298	#2307	Christmas Gold
		#3685	#70	#3089	Mauve Dk.
		#3687	#69	#3088	Mauve
		#3688	#68	#3087	Mauve Med.
		#3726	#970	#3082	Antique Mauve Dk.

Psalm 23

Designed by Craig & Laura Scott

MATERIALS;

16" x 19" piece of lt. blue 14-count Aida; 1 yd. 45" fabric; 1⅓ yds. white 2½"-wide flat eyelet; 1⅝ yds. narrow piping; 12" x 16" pillow form

INSTRUCTIONS:

1: Center and stitch design, using two strands floss for Cross Stitch and one strand floss for Backstitch and French Knots.

NOTES: Trim stitched Aida to 13" x 17" for front.

From fabric, cut one 13" x 17" piece for back and three 6½" x 41" strips for ruffle.

2: For ruffle, with right sides together and with ½" seams, stitch 6½" x 41" strips together at short edges, forming ring. Fold in half lengthwise with wrong sides together; press. Stitch short edges of eyelet together, forming ring. Place on top of fabric ring; baste together and gather along unfinished edges to fit around front. Stitch to front, first piping, then ruffle.

Continued on next page

Psalm 23

Psalm 23
Continued from page 145

3: With right sides together and with ½" seams, stitch front and back together, being careful not to catch outside edge of ruffle in seam and leaving one edge open. Trim seam and turn right side out; press. Insert pillow form; slip stitch opening closed.❖

Stitch Count:
183 wide x 138 high

Approximate Design Size:
11-count 16⅝" x 12⅝"
14-count 13⅛" x 9⅞"
16-count 11½" x 8⅝"
18-count 10¼" x 7¾"
22-count 8⅜" x 6⅜"

X	B'st	¼x	Fr	DMC	ANCHOR	J.&P. COATS	COLORS
			●	#209	#109	#4303	Lavender Med.
				#310	#403	#8403	Black
			●	#445	#288	#2288	Lemon Lt.
				#453	#231	#8397	Shell Grey Lt.
				#469	#267	#6261	Avocado Green Med.
				#471	#265	#6010	Avocado Green Very Lt.
				#3740	#873	#4223	Antique Violet Dk.
				#3753	#128	#7031	Blue Denim Pale
				#3787	#393	#5393	Beige Grey Very Dk.
				White	#2	#1001	White

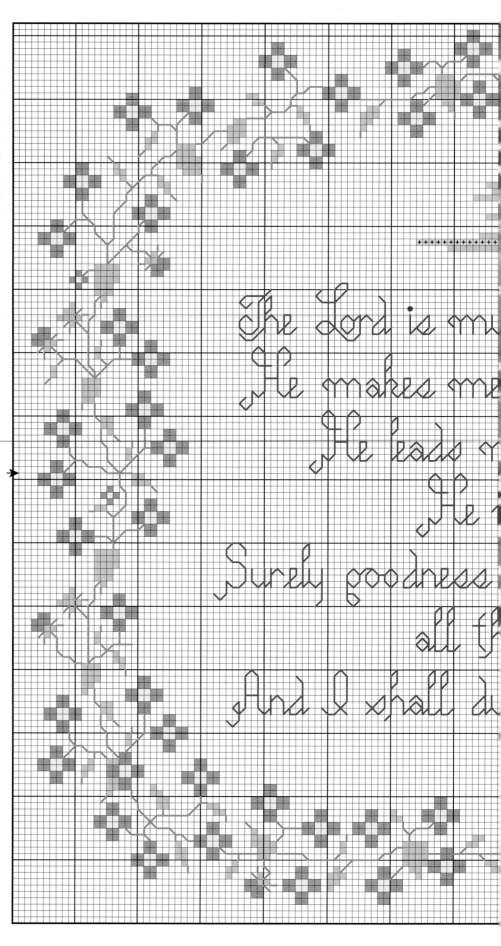

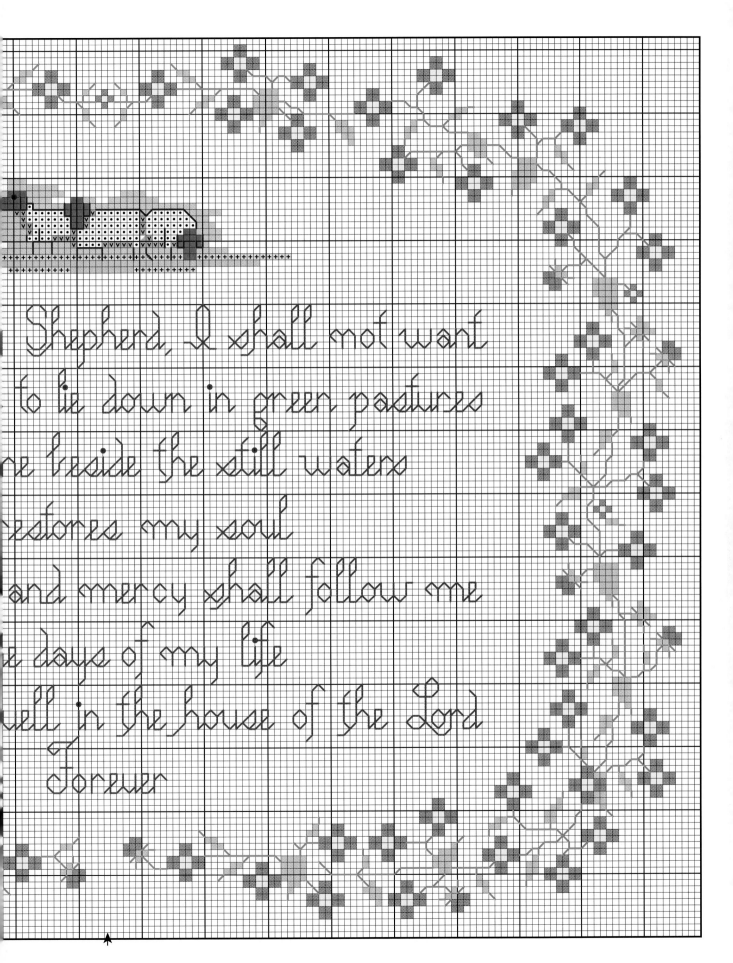

Shepherd, I shall not want
to lie down in green pastures
re beside the still waters
restores my soul
and mercy shall follow me
e days of my life
ell in the house of the Lord
Forever

Bible Verses

Designed by Stephen Wendling

MATERIALS:

One 17" x 18" piece and one 15" x 18" piece of tea-dyed 28-count Irish Linen; ¾ yd. of purple 45" fabric; ½ yd. of beige 45" fabric; 1⅝ yds. thick cording; 1½ yds. narrow cording; Craft batting; Polyester fiberfill

INSTRUCTIONS:

Pillow

1: Center and stitch design onto 17" x 18" piece of Irish linen, stitching over two threads and using two strands floss for Cross Stitch, Backstitch and French Knots of lettering. Use one strand floss for remaining Backstitch.

NOTES: Trim stitched design to 14½" x 15½". From purple fabric, cut one 14½" x 15½" piece for back and two 2½" x 31" strips for piping covering.

2: For piping, stitch 2½" x 31" strips together along short edges forming one long strip. Fold strip in half lengthwise with wrong sides together and with cording between; stitch together using a zipper foot.

3: With right sides together and with ½" seams, stitch piping around outside edge of Pillow front. With right sides together, stitch Pillow back and front together, leaving an opening; trim seams. Turn right

side out; press. Fill with fiberfill and slip stitch opening closed.

Bible Cover

NOTE: Measure Bible, and chart desired border design onto graph paper to assure correct positioning, choosing flowers and motifs from graph.

1: Center and stitch design onto 15" x 18" piece of Irish linen, stitching over two threads and using two strands floss for Cross Stitch and Backstitch.

NOTES: Trim stitched design 1" larger than Bible measurement for Bible Cover. From beige fabric, cut one piece same as front and two 4" x height of Bible pieces for flaps. From purple fabric, cut two 2" x 27" strips for piping covering.

2: For piping, make same as Step 2 of Pillow. With right sides together, stitch piping around outside edge of Bible Cover front. Finish one long edge of each flap. With right sides together and with ½" seams, stitch unfinished edges of flaps to front. With right sides together and with ½" seams, stitch Bible Cover lining to front, leaving an opening. Turn right side out; press. Insert Bible into cover.❖

Graph on next page

Bible Verses

Instructions on page 149

Stitch Count:
162 wide x 150 high

Approximate Design Size:
11-count 14¾" x 13⅝"
14-count 11⅝" x 10¾"
16-count 10⅛" x 9⅜"
18-count 9" x 8⅜"
22-count 7⅜" x 6⅞"
28-count over two
   threads 11⅝" x 10¾"

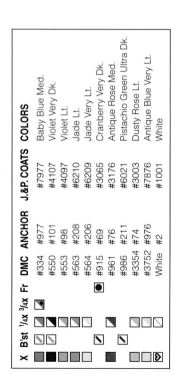

X	B'st	¼x	¾x	Fr	DMC	ANCHOR	J.&P. COATS	COLORS
					#334	#977	#7977	Baby Blue Med.
					#550	#101	#4107	Violet Very Dk.
					#553	#98	#4097	Violet Lt.
					#563	#208	#6210	Jade Lt.
					#564	#206	#6209	Jade Very Lt.
				●	#915	#69	#3065	Cranberry Very Dk.
					#961	#76	#3176	Antique Rose Med.
					#986	#211	#6021	Pistachio Green Ultra Dk.
					#3354	#74	#3003	Dusty Rose Lt.
					#3752	#976	#7876	Antique Blue Very Lt.
					White	#2	#1001	White

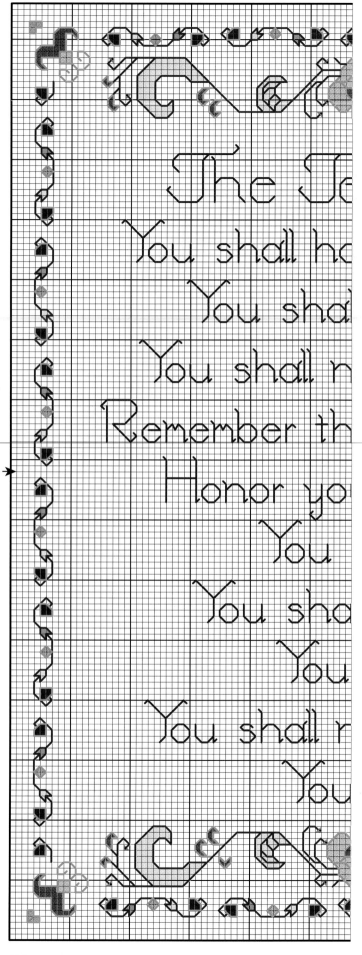

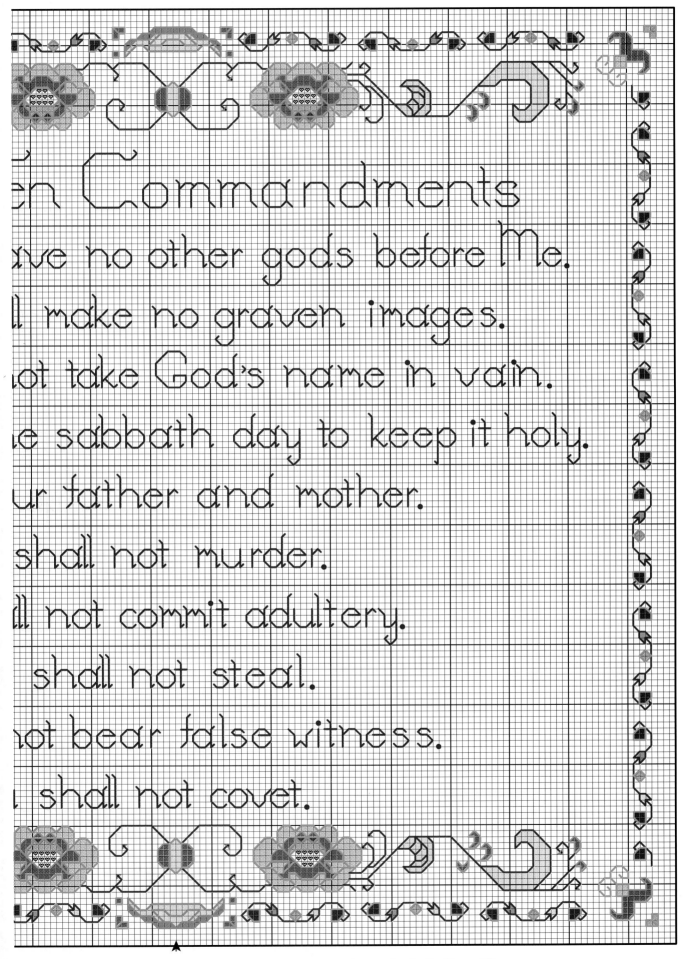

en Commandments

ve no other gods before Me.

ll make no graven images.

ot take God's name in vain.

e sabbath day to keep it holy.

ur father and mother.

shall not murder.

ll not commit adultery.

shall not steal.

ot bear false witness.

shall not covet.

Love is patient. It remains constant in the face of adversity. It is never demanding. Love speaks softly. It is never harsh or discordant. Surely with God's blessing, true love is eternal.

Love is Patient

DESIGNED BY KATHLEEN HURLEY

MATERIALS:

14" x 16" piece of daffodil 28-count Pastel linen

INSTRUCTIONS:

1: Center and stitch design, stitching over two threads and using two strands floss for Cross Stitch and one strand floss for Backstitch.❖

Graph continued on next page

Stitch Count:
132 wide x 111 high

Approximate Design Size:
11-count 12" x 10⅛"
14-count 9½" x 8"
16-count 8¼" x 7"
18-count 7⅜" x 6¼"
22-count 6" x 5⅛"
28-count over two
   threads 9½" x 8"

X	Bst	¼x	Fr	DMC	ANCHOR	J.&P. COATS	COLORS
			●	#310	#403	#8403	Black
				#326	#39	#3401	Rose Ultra Deep
				#351	#10	#3011	Coral
				#434	#370	#5000	Russet
				#699	#923	#6228	Christmas Green
				#702	#239	#6239	Parrot Green Dk.
				#704	#238	#6238	Chartreuse Bright
				#725	#305	#2298	Canary Deep
				#726	#295	#2294	Topaz Lt.
				#727	#293	#2289	Topaz Very Lt.
				#754	#6	#2331	Peach Flesh Very Lt.
				#797	#132	#7023	Blue Med.
				#799	#136	#7030	Blue
				#800	#129	#7020	Delft Pale
				#818	#23	#3281	Pink Med.
				#3326	#36	#3126	Melon Lt.
				Ecru	#387	#1002	Off White

Love is patient. It remains constant in the face of adversity. It [is] never demanding. Love [speaks] softly. It is never [discordant]. Surely [blessing], true

General Instructions

Tools of the Stitcher

FABRICS

All counted cross stitch is worked on evenweave fabric, which means the horizontal and vertical threads are of the same thickness and are equally spaced. Evenweave fabric allows the cross stitches to form neat, even squares. There are many different styles, colors and stitch counts available in evenweave fabrics.

The most popular fabric for counted cross stitch is Aida cloth. Aida is manufactured specifically for cross stitch and is available in a wide variety of colors and stitch counts from 6 to 18. Most beginning cross stitchers find Aida especially easy to work with, because the holes for stitching are clearly visible.

Linen is made from fibers of the flax plant and is strong and durable. Its lasting quality makes it the perfect choice for heirloom projects. Linen is available in a range of muted colors and stitch counts from 18 to 50. The weave of linen is finer than the weave of Aida cloth, and each cross stitch is worked over two threads.

Perforated paper and plastic are also used for cross stitching.

NEEDLES

A cross stitch needle should be blunt, with a long, narrow eye. It should slip easily between the threads of the fabric, but should not pierce the fabric. For most cross stitch on fabric, size 24 or 26 tapestry needles work well. Some stitchers prefer to use a slightly smaller needle for backstitching.

The needle should glide through quickly and easily, requiring almost no effort from the stitcher. If your finger is getting sore from pushing the needle, or if you don't like to stitch without a thimble, your needle may be too big.

HOOPS, FRAMES & SCISSORS

Hoops can be round or oval and come in many sizes. The three main types are plastic, spring-tension and wooden. Frames are easier on the fabric than hoops and come in many sizes and shapes. Once fabric is mounted it doesn't have to be removed until stitching is complete, saving fabric from excessive handling.

Small, sharp scissors are essential for cutting floss and removing mistakes. For cutting fabrics, invest in a top-quality pair of medium-sized sewing scissors. To keep them in top form, use these scissors only for cutting fabrics and floss.

Stitching Threads

Today's cross stitcher can achieve a vast array of effects in texture, color and shine. In addition to the perennial favorite, six-strand floss, stitchers can choose from sparkling metallics, shiny rayons, silks, narrow ribbon threads and much more.

SIX-STRAND FLOSS

Six-strand floss comes in a variety of colors and is available in silk and rayon as well as cotton. When working with floss, it is important to separate all six strands, then recombine the number of strands needed. To make separation easier and to prevent tangling, run cut strand over a damp sponge before separating.

Most projects are worked using two or three strands of floss for cross stitches and one or two strands for backstitches. For ease of stitching and to prevent wear on fibers, use lengths no longer than 18".

PEARL COTTON & WOOL YARN

Pearl cotton is available in #3, #5 and #8, with #3 being the thickest. The plies of pearl cotton will not separate, and for most stitching one strand is used. Pearl cotton has a lustrous sheen.

Three-ply Persian wool can be separated into one ply for use on cross stitch fabrics with a low stitch count, such as 11-count Aida and 6-count afghan fabric.

FLOWER & RIBBON THREADS

Flower thread has a tight twist and comes in many soft colors. It is heavier than one ply of six-strand floss – one strand of flower thread equals two strands of floss. Ribbon thread is a narrow ribbon especially created for stitching. It comes in a large number of colors in satin as well as metallic finishes.

BLENDING FILAMENT

Blending filament is a fine, shiny fiber that can be used alone or combined with floss or other thread. Knotting the blending filament on the needle with a slipknot is recommended for control.

SLIPKNOT

STITCHING WITH BEADS

Small seed beads can be added to any 11- or 14-count cross stitch design, using one bead per stitch. Knot thread at beginning of beaded section for security, especially if you are adding beads to clothing. The bead should lie in the same direction as the top half of cross stitches.

BEAD ATTACHMENT

Use one strand floss to secure beads. Bring needle up from back of work leaving 2" length of thread hanging, do not knot (end will be secured between stitches as you work), thread bead on needle; complete stitch.

Do not skip over more than two stitches or spaces without first securing thread, or last bead will be loose. To secure, weave thread into several stitches on back of work.

Before You Begin

Assemble fabric, floss pattern and tools. Familiarize yourself with the graph, color key and instructions before beginning.

PREPARING FABRIC

Before you stitch, decide how large to cut fabric. If you are making a pillow or other design which requires a large unstitched area, be sure to leave plenty of fabric. If you are making a small project, leave at least 3" around all edges of design. Determine the design area size by using this formula: number of stitches across design area divided by the number of threads per inch of fabric equals size of fabric in inches. Measure fabric, then cut evenly along horizontal and vertical threads.

Press out folds. To prevent raveling, hand overcast or machine zigzag fabric edges. Find center of fabric by folding horizontally and vertically, and mark with a small stitch.

READING GRAPHS

Cross stitch graphs may be black and white with symbols only, color only, or a combination of color and symbols. Each square represents one cross stitch over one square on Aida cloth or two or more threads on evenweave. Each graph has a color key, indicating which color floss and what type of stitch corresponds with each color or symbol.

Color keys have abbreviated headings for cross stitch (x), one-half cross stitch (½x), quarter cross stitch (¼x), three-quarter cross stitch (¾x) and backstitch (B'st). Also included are color numbers for several popular brands of floss. Whenever used, abbreviations for blending filament (BF) and pearl cotton (PC) will also be included. Some graphs are so large they must be divided for printing.

PREPARING FLOSS

The six strands of floss are easily separated, and the number of strands used is given in instructions.

Cut strands in 14"-18" lengths. When separating floss, always separate all six strands, then recombine the number of strands needed. To make floss separating easier, run cut length across a damp sponge. To prevent floss from tangling, run cut length through a fabric-softener dryer sheet before separating and threading needle. To colorfast red floss tones, which sometimes bleed, hold floss under running water until water runs clear. Allow to air dry.

Stitching Techniques

BEGINNING & ENDING A THREAD

Begin stitching by bringing your needle up from the underside of fabric at starting point. There are two ways to secure those first stitches. Try each one and decide which one is best for you.

1: Securing the thread. Start by pulling needle through fabric back to front, leaving about 1" behind fabric. Hold this end with fingers as you begin stitch, and work over end with your first few stitches. After work is in progress, weave end through the back of a few stitches.

2: Loop stitch. This method can only be used for even numbers of strands. Cut strands twice the normal length, then take half the number of strands needed and fold in half. Insert loose ends in needle and bring needle up from back at first stitch, leaving loop underneath. Take needle down through fabric and through loop; pull to secure.

For even stitches, keep a consistent tension on your thread and pull thread and needle completely through fabric with each stab of the needle. Make all the top crosses on your cross stitches face the same direction. To finish a thread, run the needle under the back side of several stitches and clip. Threads carried across the back of unworked areas may show through to the front, so do not carry threads.

MASTER STITCHERY

Work will be neater if you always try to make each stitch by coming up in an unoccupied hole and going down in an occupied hole.

The sewing method is preferred for stitching on linen and some other evenweaves but can also be used on Aida. Stitches are made as in hand sewing

WORKING ON EVENWEAVE: When working on linen or other evenweave fabric, keep needle on right side of fabric, taking needle front to back to front with each stitch. Work over two threads, placing the beginning and end of the bottom half of the first Cross Stitch where a vertical thread crosses a horizontal thread.

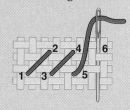

with needle going from front to back to front of fabric in one motion. All work is done from the front of the fabric. When stitching with the sewing method, it is important not to pull thread too tightly or stitches will become distorted. Stitching on linen is prettiest with the sewing method, using no hoop. If you use a hoop or frame when using the sewing method with Aida, keep in mind that fabric cannot be pulled taut. There must be "give" in the fabric in order for needle to slip in and out easily.

In the stab method, needle and floss are taken completely through fabric twice with each stitch. For the first half of the stitch, bring needle up and pull thread completely through fabric to the front. Then take needle down and reach underneath and pull completely through to bottom.

Basic Stitchery
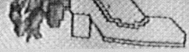

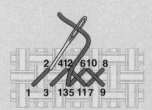

CROSS STITCH (x): There are two ways of making a basic Cross Stitch. The first method is used when working rows of stitches in the same color. The first step makes the bottom half of the stitches across the row, and the second step makes the top half.

The second method is used when making single stitches. The bottom and top halves of each stitch are worked before starting the next stitch.

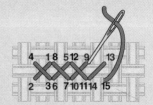

HALF CROSS STITCH (½x): The first part of a cross stitch. May slant in either direction.

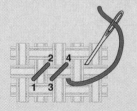

QUARTER CROSS STITCH (¼x): Stitch may slant in any direction.

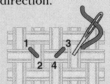

THREE-QUARTER CROSS STITCH (¾x): A Half Cross Stitch plus a Quarter Cross Stitch. May slant in any direction.

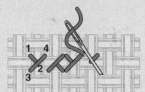

PERFORATED PAPER & PLASTIC

When cutting perforated plastic, cut on outside edge of bar preceding first stitch.
Do not count holes.

| CUTTING ILLUSTRATION | CONTINENTAL STITCH | WHIPSTITCH | OVERCAST |

Embellishing With Embroidery

EMBROIDERY stitches add detail and dimension to stitching. Unless otherwise noted, work backstitches first, then other embroidery stitches.

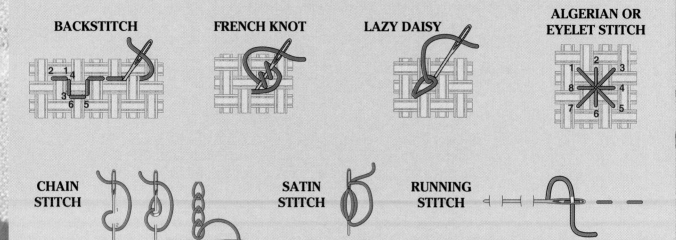

BACKSTITCH · FRENCH KNOT · LAZY DAISY · ALGERIAN OR EYELET STITCH

CHAIN STITCH · SATIN STITCH · RUNNING STITCH

Washing, Drying & Blocking Your Needlework

Careful washing and pressing help preserve and protect your stitched piece. After stitching is complete, a gentle washing will remove surface dirt, hoop marks and hand oils that have accumulated on your fabric while stitching. Even if a piece looks clean, it's always a good idea to give it a nice cleaning before finishing. Never press your work before cleaning, as this only serves to set those hoop marks and soils that are best removed.

Using a gentle soap such as baby shampoo or gentle white dishwashing liquid and a large, clean bowl, make a solution of cool, sudsy water. If you use a handwash product, make sure the one you choose contains no chlorine bleach. Fill another bowl or sink with plain cool water for rinsing.

Soak your stitched piece in sudsy water for five to ten minutes. Then gently and without rubbing or twisting, squeeze suds through fabric several times. Dip piece several times in fresh cool water until no suds remain.

On rare occasions floss colors will run or fade slightly. When this happens, continue to rinse in cool water until water becomes perfectly clear. Remove fabric from water and lay on a soft, white towel. Never twist or wring your work. Blot excess water away and roll the piece up in the towel, pressing gently.

Never allow a freshly washed piece of embroidery to air dry. Instead, remove the damp piece from the towel and place face down on a fresh, dry white towel. To prevent color stains, it's important to keep the stitched piece flat, not allowing stitched areas to touch each other or other areas of the fabric. Make sure the edges of fabric are in straight lines and even. To be sure fabric edges are straight when pressing dry, use a ruler or T-square to check edges. Wash towel several times before using it to block cross stitch, and use it only for this purpose.

After edges are aligned and fabric is perfectly smooth, cover the back of the stitched piece with a pressing cloth, cotton diaper or other lightweight white cotton cloth. Press dry with a dry iron set on a high permanent press or cotton setting, depending on fabric content. Allow stitchery to lie in this position several hours. Machine drying is acceptable after use for items like towels and kitchen accessories, but your work will be prettier and smoother if you give these items a careful pressing the first time.

Framing

SHOPPING FOR FRAMES

When you shop for a frame, take the stitchery along with you and compare several frame and mat styles. Keep in mind the "feeling" of your stitched piece when choosing a frame. For example, an exquisite damask piece stitched with metallics and silk threads might need an ornate gold frame, while a primitive sampler stitched on dirty linen with flower thread would need a simpler, perhaps wooden frame.

MOUNTING

Cross stitch pieces can be mounted on mat board, white cardboard, special padded or un-padded mounting boards designed specifically for needlework, or special acid-free mat board available from art supply stores. Acid-free framing materials are the best choice for projects you wish to keep well-preserved for future generations. If you prefer a padded look, cut quilt batting to fit mounting board.

Center blocked stitchery over mounting board of choice with quilt batting between, if desired. Leaving 1½" to 3" around all edges, trim excess fabric away along straight grain.

Mounting boards made for needlework have self-stitch surfaces and require no pins. When using these products, lift and smooth needlework onto board until work is taut and edges are smooth and even. Turn board face down and smooth fabric to back, mitering corners.

Pins are required for other mounting boards. With design face up, keeping fabric straight and taut, insert a pin through fabric and edge of mounting board at the center of each side. Turn piece face down and smooth excess fabric to back, mitering corners.

There are several methods for securing fabric edges. Edges may be glued to mat board with liquid fabric glue or fabric glue stick. If mat board is thick, fabric may be stapled.

MATS & GLASS

Pre-cut mats are available in many sizes and colors to fit standard-size frames. Custom mats are available in an even wider variety of colors, textures and materials. Using glass over cross stitch is a matter of personal preference, but is generally discouraged. Moisture can collect behind glass and rest on fabric, causing mildew stains. A single or double mat will hold glass away from fabric.

Fine Finishing Techniques

HEMMING

For a narrow double-fold hem, trim edges evenly. Then turn under edge ¼", then ¼" more. Finger press and hand baste, mitering corners. Sew with tiny hand stitches or machine topstitch with matching or contrasting thread. To add lace to a simple hem, baste gathered or flat lace under edge of hem and hand or machine-stitch in place.

FINE HEMSTITCHING

For fine evenweave cross stitch pieces, a drawn hemstitch border above a simple, narrow hem adds an heirloom touch.

Trim fabric edges even. Carefully remove four threads ½" from edge. To work the drawn hemstitch, see Steps 1-3 below. Hem by hand as above.

FINE HEMSTITCHING

STEP 1: Thread needle with thread removed from fabric; re-weave corners. Working from wrong side, with one strand floss, insert needle at point A, go under two threads and come up at point B. Insert needle at point A and come up at point C; pull securely.

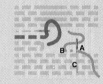

STEP 2: Repeat Step 1 sequence over four threads. Repeat across. Weave in loose ends.

STEP 3: Work across opposite side of drawn area in same manner, alternating threads as shown, forming drawn thread pattern.

Index